The Ethics of Abortion

Christine Watkins, *Book Editor*

Bruce Glassman, *Vice President*
Bonnie Szumski, *Publisher*
Helen Cothran, *Managing Editor*

GREENHAVEN PRESS
An imprint of Thomson Gale, a part of The Thomson Corporation

Detroit • New York • San Francisco • San Diego • New Haven, Conn.
Waterville, Maine • London • Munich

© 2005 Thomson Gale, a part of The Thomson Corporation.

Thomson and Star Logo are trademarks and Gale and Greenhaven Press are registered trademarks used herein under license.

For more information, contact
Greenhaven Press
27500 Drake Rd.
Farmington Hills, MI 48331-3535
Or you can visit our Internet site at http://www.gale.com

LIBRARY OF CONGRESS CATALOGING-IN-PUBLICATION DATA

The ethics of abortion / Christine Watkins, book editor.
   p. cm. — (At issue)
Includes bibliographical references and index.
ISBN 0-7377-2709-8 (lib. bdg. : alk. paper) —
ISBN 0-7377-2710-1 (pbk. : alk. paper)
   1. Abortion—Moral and ethical aspects. 2. Abortion—United States.
I. Watkins, Christine, 1951– . II. At issue (San Diego, Calif.)
HQ767.15.E48 2005
179'.6—dc22
                                                      2005045119

Printed in the United States of America

Contents

Introduction

The abortion debate is as passionate today as it was in 1973 when the Supreme Court's decision in the case of *Roe v. Wade* established a woman's right to have an abortion. For most people on both sides of the abortion controversy, the debate revolves around one critical focal point: the personhood of the fetus. As philosopher and author Peter Kreeft explains, "Persons have a 'right to life' but non-persons (e.g., cells, tissues, organs, and animals) do not. . . . If the fetus is not a person, abortion is not the deliberate killing of an innocent person; if it is, it is." So the crux of the abortion debate is whether or not a fetus inside the womb should be considered a person, with all inherent rights.

Most people who advocate legal abortion are not pro-abortion. Their objectives are the same as that of abortion opponents: to reduce the number of abortions performed and to make any necessary abortion safe. The two groups also agree that once human personhood begins, the person has a fundamental right to life and must be protected. But the two sides vehemently disagree about the point at which human personhood begins.

Nearly all opponents of abortion, or "pro-lifers," believe human personhood begins at conception. As C. Ward Kischer, professor of anatomy and human embryology, declares, "Every human embryologist, worldwide, states that the life of the new individual human being begins at fertilization (conception). . . . We exist as a continuum of human life, which begins at fertilization and continues until death." The primary goal of the pro-life movement is to protect the right to life of the unborn.

On the other side of the debate, most supporters of legalized abortion, or "pro-choicers," believe that human personhood begins later in gestation—at viability (when the fetus can survive outside the mother's womb) or at birth. They view abortion at any time before this point as a private choice that women should have the right to make, free from government interference. This view is expressed by Caitlin Borgmann and Catherine Weiss of the American Civil Liberties Union's Reproductive Freedom Project:

5

> A woman deciding whether to continue a pregnancy stands on moral ground. She is entitled to make her decision. . . . No one else—and certainly not the government—should decide whether she will use her body to bring new life into the world. The decision is too intimate and too important to be taken from her.

Though the pro-choice and pro-life views seem clearly delineated, the controversies surrounding abortion seem to be growing increasingly complex with advances in medicine and biotechnology. However, the question of personhood remains at the center of many of these debates. For example, whereas once the primary question facing a woman considering abortion was whether or not to have the child, now she may also consider what kind of child she will have. Increasingly sophisticated genetic tests can detect Down syndrome, the fatal Tay-Sachs disease, and other serious birth defects in the fetus. Many pregnant women who discover they are carrying an abnormal fetus elect to abort that fetus.

This method of targeting and eliminating disabled fetuses horrifies many disability rights activists. According to Wellesley College professor Adrienne Asch, there is an implicit message in the practice of abortion based on genetic characteristics: "It is better not to exist than to have a disability. . . . Your family and the world would be better off without you alive." Pro-choice advocates, on the other hand, see an important moral distinction between a fetus with disabilities and a baby born and living with disabilities. They maintain that selective abortion is a morally reasonable means of preventing disabling traits.

For both sides, the question of the personhood of the fetus is central to the issue. Pro-choicers support selective abortion because they do not believe that the embryo or fetus is a person yet. Conversely, pro-lifers condemn selective abortion precisely because they believe that the embryo or fetus is a person, regardless of genetic defects, and therefore should be respected and protected.

Stem cell research is another advance in human biotechnology that appears to complicate the abortion issue. Embryos have cells called stem cells that can develop into almost any type of cell. Researchers believe that stem cells can be used to treat devastating diseases such as Parkinson's or Alzheimer's, and can help improve cancer treatments and spinal cord injuries. Recent polls show that almost 60 percent of people who resolutely oppose abortion support stem cell research, even though the cells often come from aborted fetuses. As Edith Newton, whose husband suffers from the incurable Lou Gehrig's disease, puts it, "Those babies were going to be aborted regardless of what my beliefs are. It would be no different if a murder victim's family donated his organs. Are you going to say, 'No, I don't need his heart because somebody killed him'? I don't think so."

Although the debate over stem cell research has its own complexities, one of its central controversies—like so many issues related to abortion—involves personhood of the fetus. Because it views the embryo as a person, the Roman Catholic Church teaches that embryonic research violates the pro-life ethic. At the opposite end of the spectrum, many supporters of stem cell research view the embryo as merely a clump of cells and therefore believe that using such cells for research is not only justifiable but a moral good in itself.

Without a clear-cut definition of human personhood and the point at which it begins, it may be impossible to resolve the ethical issues surrounding abortion. A consensus among religious, academic, and social groups, as well as the entire American population, is far from occurring. The viewpoints in *At Issue: The Ethics of Abortion* reflect various perspectives on this controversial subject. The issue of abortion has been passionately debated in the three decades since *Roe v. Wade*, and will likely remain controversial for decades to come.

1

Abortion Is a Woman's Right

Center for Reproductive Rights

The Center for Reproductive Rights is a nonprofit legal advocacy organization dedicated to promoting and defending women's reproductive rights worldwide.

International human rights agreements support a woman's right to make decisions that affect her own body. Among these rights are the right to physical integrity, which entitles her to decide if she will or will not carry a pregnancy to term; the right to privacy, which allows her to decide to have an abortion without government interference; the right to life, under which she should have access to a medically safe abortion that will not endanger her life. If a woman decides that an abortion is in her best interest, governments should respect that decision and recognize that she is exercising her basic human rights.

Each year, 75 million women have unwanted pregnancies. Each of these women has her own familial relationships, hopes for the future, economic concerns, and health needs. These and other factors will influence her decision either to carry a pregnancy to term or to seek an abortion. Given the complexity of this decision, the only person equipped to make it is the pregnant woman herself. Neither family, nor clergy, nor community, nor government has the capacity to make that decision for her.

Governments should respect a woman's human right to

make decisions regarding her reproductive life. A woman who decides to have an abortion must have access to the facilities and care that will enable her to terminate her pregnancy safely. Governments that prosecute and punish women who have had abortions penalize women for exercising their basic rights. These rights are no less compromised when a woman who decides to terminate a pregnancy can do so only by undertaking a serious risk to her health. . . .

Abortion Is a Woman's Choice

A woman has a right to make decisions regarding her own body. Support for this right is found in a number of human rights instruments, which contain provisions that ensure freedom in decision-making about private matters. Such provisions include protections of the right to physical integrity, the right to decide freely and responsibly the number and spacing of one's children, and the right to privacy.

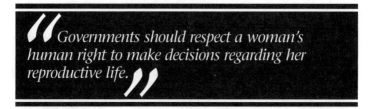

Governments should respect a woman's human right to make decisions regarding her reproductive life.

Women have the right to decide whether or not to bring a pregnancy to term.

- The *right to physical integrity* ensures freedom from unwanted invasions of one's body. When a pregnancy is unwanted, its continuation can take a heavy toll on a woman's physical and emotional well-being. A woman's right to physical integrity entitles her to decide whether or not she will carry a pregnancy to term.
- A woman's *right to determine the number and spacing of her children* requires governments to make abortion services legal, safe, and accessible to all women. Women are entitled to have access to all safe, effective means of controlling their family size, including abortion. In addition, there are a number of circumstances in which abortion may be a woman's only means of exercising her right to plan her family. A woman who becomes pregnant through an act of non-consensual sex would be forced to bear a child were

she denied her right to an abortion. For women who live in settings in which family planning services and education are unavailable, access to safe abortion services may be the only means of controlling their family size. Finally, contraceptive failure will inevitably occur among some of those women who regularly use contraception.

- Decisions one makes about one's body, particularly one's reproductive capacity, lie squarely in the domain of private decision-making. A woman's *right to privacy*, therefore, entitles her to decide whether or not to undergo an abortion without government interference. Only a pregnant woman knows whether she is ready to have a child, and governments can play no role in influencing that decision.

Abortion Bans Discriminate Against Women

The right to gender equality is a fundamental principle of human rights law. Freedom from discrimination in the enjoyment of protected human rights is ensured in every major human rights instrument.

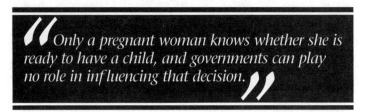

Only a pregnant woman knows whether she is ready to have a child, and governments can play no role in influencing that decision.

Denying women access to abortion is a form of gender discrimination.

- According to the Convention on the Elimination of All Forms of Discrimination against Women, "discrimination against women" includes laws that have either the "effect" or the "purpose" of preventing a woman from exercising any of her human rights or fundamental freedoms on a basis of equality with men. *Laws that ban abortion have just that effect and that purpose.*
- Restricting abortion has the *effect* of denying women access to a procedure that may be necessary for their enjoyment of their right to health. Only women must live with the physical and emotional consequences of unwanted pregnancy. Some women suffer maternity-related injuries, such as hemorrhage or obstructed labor. Denying women

access to medical services that enable them to regulate their fertility or terminate a dangerous pregnancy amounts to a refusal to provide health care that only women need. Women are consequently exposed to health risks not experienced by men.

- The discriminatory *purpose* of the restrictive abortion laws of a number of countries also bears examination. Laws that deny access to abortion, whatever their stated objectives, relegate women to their traditional roles as nurturers and mothers. The tendency to define women by their reproductive capacity remains highly prevalent throughout the world. Governments continue to downplay the impedance of women's participation in the areas of political, economic, social, cultural, and civil affairs. In contrast, societies that have welcomed women's participation in affairs outside the home have increasingly recognized that reproductive decision-making is best left to women themselves.

Women's Right to Health
Entitles Them to Safe Abortion

International law guarantees women the right to "the highest attainable standard of health." Unsafe abortion can have devastating effects on women's health. Where death does not result from unsafe abortion, women may experience long-term disabilities, such as uterine perforation, chronic pelvic pain, or pelvic inflammatory disease.

Safe abortion services protect women's right to health.

- The World Health Organization defines "health" as "a state of complete physical, mental and social well-being, not merely the absence of disease or infirmity." While the right to health does not guarantee perfect health for all women, it has been interpreted to require governments to provide health care and to work toward creating conditions conducive to the enjoyment of good health. In the context of abortion, this right to health can be interpreted to require governments to take appropriate measures to ensure that women are not exposed to the risks of unsafe abortion. Such measures include removing legal restrictions on abortion and ensuring access to high-quality abortion services.
- The Programme of Action adopted at the International Conference on Population and Development (ICPD) called upon governments to consider the consequences of unsafe

abortion on women's health. It states that governments should "deal with the health impact of unsafe abortion as a major public health concern."

- At the 1995 Fourth World Conference on Women, the international community reiterated this language and urged governments to "consider reviewing laws containing punitive measures against women who have undergone illegal abortions." In addition, in a paragraph addressing research on women's health, the Platform for Action urges governments "to understand and better address the determinants and consequences of unsafe abortion."

Unsafe Abortion Threatens Women's Right to Life

The right to life is protected in multiple human rights instruments. It is widely acknowledged that in countries in which abortion is legally restricted, women seek abortions clandestinely, under conditions that are medically unsafe and therefore life-threatening. According to the World Health Organization, unsafe abortions are responsible for the deaths of 78,000 women each year.

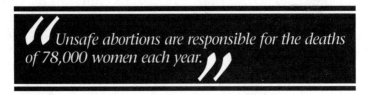

Unsafe abortions are responsible for the deaths of 78,000 women each year.

Forcing a woman to undergo an unsafe abortion violates her right to life.

- Because unsafe abortion is closely associated with high rates of maternal mortality, laws that force women to resort to unsafe procedures infringe upon women's *right to life*.
- While the phrase "right to life" has been associated with the campaigns of those who oppose abortion, it has not been interpreted in an international setting to require restrictions on abortion.

2

Abortion Violates the Unborn Child's Right to Life

The Society of Jesus in the United States

The Society of Jesus, commonly known as the Jesuits, is the largest religious order of the Roman Catholic Church.

The Catholic Church is committed to the value and dignity of all human life and seeks to end abortion because the fetus is a living human being. Abortion is a human rights issue as well as a social and moral issue and therefore should not be viewed as a private decision. The pro-life movement supports women so that they will respect themselves and the life of their unborn child. The Catholic Church hopes that with continued teaching and discussion, the message will reach everyone that respect for life, especially for unborn children, is of utmost importance.

In this statement we wish to underscore the correctness of Catholic Church teaching regarding abortion, joining with many other people of conscience who are working to protect life in the womb, and who are seeking an end to abortion so as to restore our country's respect for the core human value of the right to life. We wish to add further insights to support this teaching, drawing upon the heritage of our Jesuit history and the treasure of Ignatian spirituality.

In 1995, representative Jesuits from around the world met in Rome for the 34th General Congregation of the Society of Je-

The Society of Jesus in the United States, "Standing for the Unborn: A Statement of the Society of Jesus in the United States on Abortion," *America*, March 2003. Copyright © 2003 by the Jesuit Conference. Reproduced by permission.

sus. In their completed document "Our Mission and Justice," they noted that "Human life, a gift of God, has to be respected from its beginning to its natural end". The most fundamental building block of a just social order is respect for human life. Until men and women individually and collectively make a profound commitment to the value and dignity of all human life, we will never find the true peace, justice and reconciliation God desires for us.

Abortion is a key social evil.

When we, the leadership of the Society of Jesus in the U.S., survey the developments unfolding in our culture, we are deeply distressed at the massive injustices. A spirit of callous disregard for life shows itself in direct assaults on human life such as abortion and capital punishment, as well as in senseless violence, escalating militarism, racism, xenophobia, and the skewed accumulation of wealth and life-sustaining resources. These realities compel us to speak out against what Pope John Paul II has called "the culture of death."

This [year, 2003] is the 30th anniversary year of the Supreme Court decision that made abortion legal throughout the United States. Since the January 22, 1973 Supreme Court decisions in *Roe v. Wade* and *Doe v. Bolton*, more than 39 million American lives have been ended by abortion. Among all the justice issues we as a society should view with grave concern, abortion is a key social evil.

Jesuits draw upon a long and rich tradition of reflection, professional study, experience, and spirituality that brings many resources to the complexities of the abortion issue.

Abortion Affects Everyone

We offer the following insights for shaping future public dialogue about abortion:

First, abortion is a human rights issue. It is also a social issue, and not simply a personal decision made in artificial isolation from wider social reality. Attempts to frame the issue as merely a question of personal preference or private choice ignore important features of abortion as a public policy. Because the state and society as a whole have an intense interest in promoting respect for life, we may not with a clear conscience relegate such life-and-death issues to the private realm, no matter how appealing and convenient such arguments may appear on the surface. Abortion policy contains embedded cultural assumptions, values and attitudes that have wide repercussions for the way we collectively treat all human life. The whole array of potential threats to life and human dignity is interrelated, and the Christian imperative to oppose it calls forth from us a consistent ethic of life.

Second, when we as religious leaders speak out against abortion, we are in no way endangering important Constitutional principles. While we invoke faith-based claims for opposing legalized abortion, Jesuits are only one part of a broader coalition that finds many reasons to protect unborn life. In recent years, new evidence about prenatal biology has persuaded numerous people, often without explicit religious commitments, that the fetus is indeed a living, unique human being, worthy of the respect and protection we give to all human beings. When abortion laws are changed, it will not be the imposition of a narrowly confined religious position upon an unwilling majority, but rather the consequence of a new broad-based consensus grounded upon persuasive and reasonable arguments accessible to people of all faith traditions and people of none.

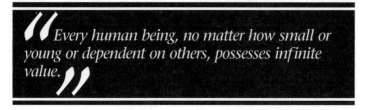

Every human being, no matter how small or young or dependent on others, possesses infinite value.

Third, beyond the actual content of "what" we say in making a case against abortion, it is critical to pay attention to "how" our defense of the unborn proceeds. As St. Paul reminds us, we must "speak the truth with love." The dialogue should never devolve into a shrill clash of shouts, much less threats of violence. We should remain confident that adjudication on the grounds of what is reasonable and consistent with human well-being is possible.

As Jesuits we now offer some observations: first, what our Catholic faith tradition teaches regarding the sanctity of all human life; second, what our distinctive Jesuit approach, including the heritage of Ignatian spirituality, brings to bear on life issues; and third, some concluding reflections on the manner of public dialogue about abortion in a pluralistic society. We hope that each will help clarify the urgency of our renewed stance in defense of human life.

The Sanctity of Human Life

The social teachings of the Catholic Church place the dignity of the human person at the center of all concerns for justice. Every human being, no matter how small or young or dependent on others, possesses infinite value. The book of Genesis testifies how it pleased God to create human persons "in the image and likeness" of God (Genesis 1:26) as free and rational beings possessing innate and sacred dignity. The Hebrew Scriptures treat violations against the life and welfare of innocent people as offenses against the God who is the Author of Life. The Decalogue unambiguously declares: "Thou shalt not kill" (Exodus 20:13).

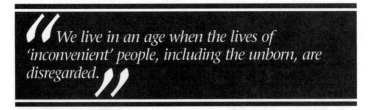

We live in an age when the lives of 'inconvenient' people, including the unborn, are disregarded.

Although the Scriptures have almost nothing to say specifically about the topic of abortion in the modern medical sense (i.e., as a surgical procedure or pharmaceutical intervention), the books of both Hebrew and Christian Scriptures paint a reality that clearly rules out disregard for innocent human life. We find in the Bible several passages that testify to the preciousness of the unborn child. The prophet Jeremiah describes God's love for the unborn: "Before I formed you in the womb, I knew you, and before you were born, I consecrated you" (Jeremiah 1:5). The book of Psalms offers this prayer of wonder: "You formed my inmost being; you knit me in my mother's womb. My very self you knew; my bones were not hidden from you, when I was being made in secret, fashioned as in the depths of the earth" (Psalm 139:13–15).

When early Christians began to reflect on their faith in Jesus of Nazareth as Christ and Lord, they concluded that abortion was a grave sin. To believe in the mystery of the Incarnation, in God's wondrous decision to become human and take on the life of our natural existence of conception, birth, maturation, and death, commits one to affirm the dignity and sacredness of human life from conception to death. One of the earliest teaching documents of the Christian community, the "Didache," circa 1st century A.D., proclaims: "Do not murder a child by abortion or kill a newborn infant." In addition, Christian reflection of subsequent eras provides an unbroken testament of an utter respect for unborn life. Though theologians of the patristic, medieval, scholastic and early modern eras offered diverse speculations on the origin and nature of the early stages of human life, Catholic tradition provides solid support and grounding for contemporary church teachings against abortion.

> **"** *Horrible trauma and regret often haunt participants in the aftermath of abortion.* **"**

Church leaders in the past century have found it necessary to reiterate the importance of the respect for life and condemnation of any violation of the right to life, the most basic value upon which all other human rights depend. We live in an age when the lives of "inconvenient" people, including the unborn, are disregarded. Demands for legalized abortion have sprouted around the globe. All the popes of the 20th century have spoken out boldly against abortion as well as a panoply of other threats to human life. The Second Vatican Council, in its 1965 social teaching document "Pastoral Constitution on the Church in the Modern World" (*Gaudium et Spes*), reminds us that "life must be safeguarded with extreme care from conception; abortion and infanticide are abominable crimes". . . .

Moral Decisions Are Often Difficult

Ignatian spirituality reminds us that the work of making correct choices about moral issues such as respect for unborn life is a difficult one. Through the Spiritual Exercises of St. Ignatius, a believer comes to realize that our lamentable hardness of heart, our sinful tendency toward selfishness and our aptitude for choosing to follow the "enemy of our human nature" make refusal to protect human dignity a real possibility even for well-intentioned people.

St. Ignatius was famous for teaching the "discernment of spirits" and urged his followers to take greater notice of their emotions, internal movements and spiritual desires. He instructs us to be attentive to the various kinds of decisions that typically confront us, including matters of clear right and wrong.

Because we support women, we oppose abortion.

These insights shed some light on the ethics of abortion, at least insofar as we might assist in discerning the psychological health and spiritual state of those who procure or undergo abortions. Evidence from numerous sources, including the Project Rachel programs set up in many dioceses to counsel women and men who have experienced or been involved with abortions, suggests at least two things. First, that tremendous pressure is often brought to bear on women facing unplanned pregnancies. Second, that horrible trauma and regret often haunt participants in the aftermath of abortion. As the United States bishops poignantly noted: *"Roe v. Wade* has left a trail of broken hearts." The struggle to achieve a sense of reconciliation with God and the aborted child often takes years to resolve, if it happens at all. . . .

Anti-Abortion Is Pro-Woman

To be pro-life is to be pro-woman. Because we support women, we oppose abortion. We realize that the prevalence of abortion on demand is a clear indication that women are not receiving the types of societal and personal support necessary to bring their pregnancies to term. As Mary Ann Glendon, the Harvard law professor who headed the Holy See's delegation to the United Nations' Fourth World Conference on Women at Beijing in 1995, stated: "All who are genuinely committed to the advancement of women can and must offer a woman or a girl who is pregnant, frightened, and alone a better alternative than the destruction of her own unborn child."

Just as Jesus sought out opportunities to reach out to women who were downtrodden, challenging the social conventions of his day, so has the Society of Jesus worked with and for women since its founding. St. Ignatius worked with women of faith throughout his life, accepting their offerings when he was a destitute pilgrim and working for their advancement locally in his years in Rome and universally through the men he missioned around the world. In our day, the 34th General Congregation stated its firm resolve to oppose any social injustice based on gender, reflecting the best of this relationship between women and the Society of Jesus throughout the world in its Decree 14, "Jesuits and the Situation of Women in Church and Civil Society."

> *Our long-term goal remains full legal recognition of and protection for the unborn child—from the moment of conception.*

Some influential voices posit a zero-sum conflict between "women's reproductive rights" and the right to life of unborn children. Jesuits ought to find their place among those who demonstrate the obvious confluence of women's rights and respect for life in all its forms. Pope John Paul II summed this partnership up when he wrote: "Therefore, in firmly rejecting 'pro-choice' it is necessary to become courageously 'pro-woman,' promoting a choice that is truly in favor of women. It is precisely the woman, in fact, who pays the highest price, not only for her motherhood, but even more for its destruction, for the suppression of the life of the child who has been conceived. The only honest stance, in these cases, is that of radical solidarity with the woman. It is not right to leave her alone."

Civil Law vs. Moral Law

The United States is blessed to be a pluralistic society with a vigorous tradition of free thought and speech. To be surrounded by such a kaleidoscope of cultures, customs and ideas is a privilege rare in human history. While enriching, this can also be a potential source of frustration and conflict. What binds the United States together is a tradition of tolerance and mutual respect for the opinions of others, as guaranteed by the Bill of

Rights in the Constitution of the United States.

As Catholics and Jesuits, we would naturally prefer to live in a country where every citizen, voter, and court consistently favor legal recognition of and protection for the unborn. We are encouraged by recent evidence indicating a modest shift of public opinion away from the easy availability of abortion, and are heartened that recent polls now show that far fewer Americans are willing to call themselves "pro-choice." In addition, we are also encouraged by the large influx of young Americans—those under 30, and therefore survivors of *Roe v. Wade*—who are active in pro-life efforts. . . .

Jesuits are committed to narrowing the gap between the current civil law of our nation and the demands of the moral law as we understand it. Our long-term goal remains full legal recognition of and protection for the unborn child—from the moment of conception.

In the near future, we cannot realistically expect complete agreement among all participants in the abortion debate. We must listen respectfully to others' opinions, just as we expect a fair hearing of our own arguments against abortion. Our confidence in the persuasive power of well-articulated defenses of pro-life positions sustains us, even as we acknowledge the long struggle ahead. An acceptable outcome may be a long way off, although building a consensus against the most egregious wrongs, such as partial-birth abortions, may be possible sooner than we expect. In the meantime, our common calling is to stand in solidarity with the unborn, the "least of our brothers and sisters" (Matthew 25:40), through prayer and political activism.

As we have throughout our nearly five hundred year history, Jesuits will continue to undertake a broad variety of works and play diverse roles in the Church and in the wider society. It is our desire that Jesuits, along with their colleagues, will continue to offer a consistent message of respect for life, especially for unborn children. All of God's daughters and sons, particularly the most vulnerable and those yet to be born, must be treated with respect and protected by the laws of our nation.

3

Human Personhood Begins at Conception

Dan Kennedy

Dan Kennedy is the chief executive officer of Human Life of Washington, an affiliate of the National Right to Life Committee and the largest and longest-established pro-life educational organization in Washington State.

A human being is a person, no matter what the stage of development. At conception, the complete design of a human person exists along with the ability for development. Just as a child develops into an adult, so too will a zygote, embryo, or fetus; all are human persons, regardless of the label.

When reading or listening to the current arguments in support of cloning and the use of embryos for research, you immediately encounter arbitrary criteria masquerading as science and logic. As Professor Robert George of Princeton University has noted, the mental gymnastics required to support the destruction of embryonic human beings for research, "fails the test of reason. It requires supporters to argue that embryos are not human beings—which is contrary to fact—or that embryonic human beings are not persons—which is contrary to logic."

The arguments against personhood at conception offer particularly stunning examples of muddled thinking and convoluted logic. For example, to say that a single-celled human being at conception is no larger than the dot at the end of this sentence is to simply give a description based on appearance. It is not an explanation or definition of what this human being is. [The

Greek philosopher] Aristotle 2400 years ago noted that to obtain a true definition of what something is, you must discover what its powers are and what it is meant to be. To judge by appearance alone is both ignorant and perilous. Genocide, slavery, ethnic cleansing—history offers abundant witness to the brutal injustice that inevitably results from arbitrary judgements.

A Unique Human Being Exists at Conception

At conception each of us becomes a self-possessed human person. We possess our own future; it belongs to us uniquely and no one else. No matter our size, present within us at conception is the complete design of what we are meant to be and a guiding force or impetus that brings that development about. This power and the information necessary to direct it must be present at conception in order for development to occur.

At conception each of us becomes a self-possessed human person.

Personhood is not dependent on whether one is currently manifesting all one's powers or not. It is not a temporary state that comes and goes with our degree of functionality. A machine could conceivably be designed to look like us, and mimic numerous human traits, but functional mimicry is not personhood. Indeed, there are already machines that actually function more efficiently than we do at specific tasks, but I seriously doubt your vacuum cleaner ever wonders about the fairness of it all. You, however, are intrinsically oriented toward that unique human characteristic, evident even in young children, to desire and reflect on transcendent realities like justice and truth.

Labels Confuse the Issue

Our dignity at conception is often obscured by labels assigned to stages of development such as zygote, blastocyst, fetus, or infant. But, an embryo is not less of a human being than an infant, anymore than a child is less of a human being before puberty than after. At every stage we are whole human beings. This problem with labels is not new. In fact, Abraham Lincoln used to illustrate it by humorously asking how many legs does a dog have if you call the tail a leg? The answer is four, because it makes no difference if you call it a leg, it is still a tail. In the same way, how we label a stage of development doesn't change the fundamental nature or reality of that which we label. Tragically, language has often been engineered for the very purpose of dehumanizing those who are different, who don't look like us, or those targeted for exploitation.

Nor does the inability to perceive personhood in others serve as proof that it must not be present. One's own lack of clarity does not alter objective reality. Ironically, those who would deny personhood under these circumstances, fancy themselves more sophisticated than their historical counterparts, who condoned atrocities based on appearance. However, they display the same shallow mentality when it comes to contemporary stem cell debates. Once again we witness ignorance and utilitarian motives corrupting what is both rationally and morally obvious, that we can not earn for ourselves, or bestow on others what is already ours by nature.

Our culture's eclipse of reason has resulted in untold suffering and a relentless violation of inalienable rights. The unborn, the elderly, the disabled are all targets of these self-appointed final arbiters of personhood. Inevitably, none of us are immune from their arbitrary judgements. Healing the culture must begin with acknowledging that at conception, a unique, self-possessed human person comes into being. Their future, as well as ours, depends on it.

Human Personhood Does Not Begin at Conception

Brian Elroy McKinley

Brian Elroy McKinley is an Internet consultant and writer. His other articles include "The Big Lie" and "Why Abortion Is Biblical."

Anti-abortionists often argue that the zygote, embryo, or fetus growing inside a mother's womb is alive because it has cells that multiply and grow, and that it is human because it has human DNA. However, it is not a person because it does not have consciousness and is not able to exist on its own. Because of these factors, the fetus does not have human rights, and therefore abortion is not murder.

All of the arguments against abortion boil down to six specific questions. The first five deal with the nature of the zygote-embryo-fetus growing inside a mother's womb. The last one looks at the morality of the practice. These questions are:

1. Is it alive?
2. Is it human?
3. Is it a person?
4. Is it physically independent?
5. Does it have human rights?
6. Is abortion murder?

Let's take a look at each of these questions. We'll show how anti-abortionists use seemingly logical answers to back up their cause, but then we'll show how their arguments actually support the fact that abortion is moral.

Life vs. Personhood

1. Is it alive?

Yes. Pro Choice supporters who claim it isn't do themselves and their cause a disservice. Of course it's alive. It's a biological mechanism that converts nutrients and oxygen into energy that causes its cells to divide, multiply, and grow. It's alive.

Anti-abortion activists often mistakenly use this fact to support their cause. "Life begins at conception" they claim. And they would be right. The genesis of a new human life begins when the egg with 23 chromosomes joins with a sperm with 23 chromosomes and creates a fertilized cell, called a zygote, with 46 chromosomes. The single-cell zygote contains all the DNA necessary to grow into an independent, conscious human being. It is a potential person.

But being alive does not give the zygote full human rights—including the right not to be aborted during its gestation.

A single-cell ameba also converts nutrients and oxygen into biological energy that causes its cells to divide, multiply and grow. It also contains a full set of its own DNA. It shares everything in common with a human zygote except that it is not a potential person. Left to grow, it will always be an ameba—never a human person. It is just as alive as the zygote, but we would never defend its human rights based solely on that fact.

And neither can the anti-abortionist, which is why we must answer the following questions as well.

Being alive does not give the zygote full human rights.

2. Is it human?

Yes. Again, Pro Choice defenders stick their feet in their mouths when they defend abortion by claiming the zygote-embryo-fetus isn't human. It is human. Its DNA is that of a human. Left to grow, it will become a full human person.

And again, anti-abortion activists often mistakenly use this fact to support their cause. They are fond of saying, "an acorn is an oak tree in an early stage of development; likewise, the zygote is a human being in an early stage of development." And they would be right. But having a full set of human DNA does not give the zygote full human rights—including the right not to be aborted during its gestation.

Don't believe me? Here, try this: reach up to your head, grab one strand of hair, and yank it out. Look at the base of the hair. That little blob of tissue at the end is a hair follicle. It also contains a full set of human DNA. Granted it's the same DNA pattern found in every other cell in your body, but in reality the uniqueness of the DNA is not what makes it a different person. Identical twins share the exact same DNA, and yet we don't say that one is less human than the other, nor are two twins the exact same person. It's not the configuration of the DNA that makes a zygote human; it's simply that it has human DNA. Your hair follicle shares everything in common with a human zygote except that it is a little bit bigger and it is not a potential person. (These days even that's not an absolute considering our new-found ability to clone humans from existing DNA, even the DNA from a hair follicle.)

Your hair follicle is just as human as the zygote, but we would never defend its human rights based solely on that fact.

And neither can the anti-abortionist, which is why the following two questions become critically important to the abortion debate.

Potential Persons

3. Is it a person?

No. It's merely a potential person.

Webster's Dictionary lists a person as "being an individual or existing as an indivisible whole; existing as a distinct entity." Anti-abortionists claim that each new fertilized zygote is already a new person because its DNA is uniquely different than anyone else's. In other words, if you're human, you must be a person.

Of course we've already seen that a simple hair follicle is just as human as a single-cell zygote, and, that unique DNA doesn't make the difference since two twins are not one person. It's quite obvious, then, that something else must occur to make one human being different from another. There must be something else that happens to change a DNA-patterned body into a distinct person. (Or in the case of twins, two identically DNA-patterned bodies into two distinct persons.)

There is, and most people inherently know it, but they have trouble verbalizing it for one very specific reason.

The defining mark between something that is human and someone who is a person is 'consciousness.' It is the self-aware quality of consciousness that makes us uniquely different from others. This self-awareness, this sentient consciousness is also what separates us from every other animal life form on the planet. We think about ourselves. We use language to describe ourselves. We are aware of ourselves as a part of the greater whole.

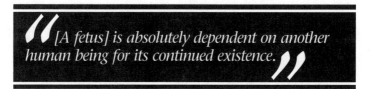

[A fetus] is absolutely dependent on another human being for its continued existence.

The problem is that consciousness normally doesn't occur until months, even years, after a baby is born. This creates a moral dilemma for the defender of abortion rights. Indeed, they inherently know what makes a human into a person, but they are also aware such individual personhood doesn't occur until well after birth. To use personhood as an argument for abortion rights, therefore, also leads to the argument that it should be okay to kill a 3-month-old baby since it hasn't obtained consciousness either.

Anti-abortionists use this perceived problem in an attempt to prove their point. In a debate, a Pro Choice defender will rightly state that the difference between a fetus and a full-term human being is that the fetus isn't a person. The anti-abortion activist, being quite sly, will reply by asking his opponent to define what makes someone into a person. Suddenly the Pro Choice defender is at a loss for words to describe what he or she knows innately. We know it because we lived it. We know we have no memory of self-awareness before our first birthday, or even before our second. But we also quickly become aware of the "problem" we create if we say a human doesn't become a person until well after its birth. And we end up saying nothing. The anti-abortionist then takes this inability to verbalize the nature of personhood as proof of their claim that a human is a person at conception.

But they are wrong. Their "logic" is greatly flawed. Just because someone is afraid to speak the truth doesn't make it any less true.

And in reality, the Pro Choice defender's fear is unfounded. They are right, and they can state it without hesitation. A human indeed does not become a full person until consciousness. And consciousness doesn't occur until well after the birth of the child. But that does not automatically lend credence to the anti-abortionist's argument that it should, therefore, be acceptable to kill a three-month-old baby because it is not yet a person.

It is still a potential person. And after birth it is an independent potential person whose existence no longer poses a threat to the physical well-being of another. To understand this better, we need to look at the next question.

4. Is it physically independent?

No. It is absolutely dependent on another human being for its continued existence. Without the mother's life-giving nutrients and oxygen it would die. Throughout gestation the zygote-embryo-fetus and the mother's body are symbiotically linked, existing in the same physical space and sharing the same risks. What the mother does affects the fetus. And when things go wrong with the fetus, it affects the mother.

Physical vs. Social Independence

Anti-abortionists claim fetal dependence cannot be used as an issue in the abortion debate. They make the point that even after birth, and for years to come, a child is still dependent on its mother, its father, and those around it. And since no one would claim its okay to kill a child because of its dependency on others, we can't, if we follow their logic, claim it's okay to abort a fetus because of its dependence.

What the anti-abortionist fails to do, however, is differentiate between physical dependence and social dependence. Physical dependence does not refer to meeting the physical needs of the child—such as in the anti-abortionist's argument above. That's social dependence; that's where the child depends on society—on other people—to feed it, clothe it, and love it. Physical dependence occurs when one life form depends solely on the physical body of another life form for its existence.

Physical dependence was cleverly illustrated back in 1971 by philosopher Judith Jarvis Thompson. She created a scenario in which a woman is kidnapped and wakes up to find she's been surgically attached to a world-famous violinist who, for nine months, needs her body to survive. After those nine months, the violinist can survive just fine on his own, but he must have this particular woman in order to survive until then.

Thompson then asks if the woman is morally obliged to stay connected to the violinist who is living off her body. It might be a very good thing if she did—the world could have the beauty that would come from such a violinist—but is she morally obliged to let another being use her body to survive?

This very situation is already conceded by anti-abortionists. They claim RU-486 should be illegal for a mother to take because it causes her uterus to flush its nutrient-rich lining, thus removing a zygote from its necessary support system and, therefore, ending its short existence as a life form. Thus the anti-abortionist's own rhetoric only proves the point of absolute physical dependence.

This question becomes even more profound when we consider a scenario where it's not an existing person who is living off the women's body, but simply a potential person, or better yet, a single-cell zygote with human DNA that is no different than the DNA in a simple hair follicle.

To complicate it even further, we need to realize that physical dependence also means a physical threat to the life of the mother. The World Health Organization reports that nearly 670,000 women die from pregnancy-related complications each year (this number does not include abortions). That's 1,800 women per day. We also read that in developed countries, such as the United States and Canada, a woman is 13 times more likely to die bringing a pregnancy to term than by having an abortion.

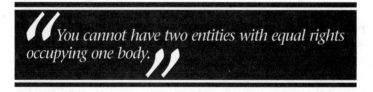

You cannot have two entities with equal rights occupying one body.

Therefore, not only is pregnancy the prospect of having a potential person physically dependent on the body of one particular woman, it also includes the woman putting herself into a life-threatening situation for that potential person.

Unlike social dependence, where the mother can choose to put her child up for adoption or make it a ward of the state or hire someone else to take care of it, during pregnancy the fetus is absolutely physically dependent on the body of one woman. Unlike social dependence, where a woman's physical life is not threatened by the existence of another person, during pregnancy, a woman places herself in the path of bodily harm for the benefit of a DNA life form that is only a potential person—even exposing herself to the threat of death.

This brings us to the next question: do the rights of a potential person supersede the rights of the mother to control her body and protect herself from potential life-threatening danger?

No Rights Prior to Birth

5. Does it have human rights?

Yes and No.

A potential person must always be given full human rights unless its existence interferes with the rights of Life, Liberty, and the Pursuit of Happiness of an already existing conscious human being. Thus, a gestating fetus has no rights before birth and full rights after birth.

If a fetus comes to term and is born, it is because the mother chooses to forgo her own rights and her own bodily security in order to allow that future person to gestate inside her body. If the mother chooses to exercise control over her own body and to protect herself from the potential dangers of childbearing, then she has the full right to terminate the pregnancy.

Anti-abortion activists are fond of saying "The only difference between a fetus and a baby is a trip down the birth canal." This flippant phrase may make for catchy rhetoric, but it doesn't belie the fact that indeed "location" makes all the difference in the world.

It's actually quite simple. You cannot have two entities with equal rights occupying one body. One will automatically have veto power over the other—and thus they don't have equal rights. In the case of a pregnant woman, giving a "right to life" to the potential person in the womb automatically cancels out the mother's right to Life, Liberty, and the Pursuit of Happiness.

After birth, on the other hand, the potential person no longer occupies the same body as the mother, and thus, giving it full human rights causes no interference with another's right to control her body. Therefore, even though a full-term human baby may still not be a person, after birth it enjoys the full support of the law in protecting its rights. After birth its independence begs that it be protected as if it were equal to a fully-conscience human being. But before birth its lack of personhood and its threat to the woman in which it resides makes abortion a completely logical and moral choice.

Abortion Is Not Murder

Which brings us to our last question, which is the real crux of the issue. . . .

6. Is abortion murder?

No. Absolutely not.

It's not murder if it's not an independent person. One might argue, then, that it's not murder to end the life of any child before she reaches consciousness, but we don't know how long after birth personhood arrives for each new child, so it's completely logical to use their independence as the dividing line for when full rights are given to a new human being.

Using independence also solves the problem of dealing with premature babies. Although a preemie is obviously still only a potential person, by virtue of its independence from the mother, we give it the full rights of a conscious person. This saves us from setting some other arbitrary date of when we consider a new human being a full person. Older cultures used to set it at two years of age, or even older. Modern religious cultures want to set it at conception, which is simply wishful thinking on their part. As we've clearly demonstrated, a single-cell zygote is no more a person than a human hair follicle.

But that doesn't stop religious fanatics from dumping their judgements and their anger on top of women who choose to exercise the right to control their bodies. It's the ultimate irony that people who claim to represent a loving God resort to scare tactics and fear to support their mistaken beliefs.

It's even worse when you consider that most women who have an abortion have just made the most difficult decision of their life. No one thinks abortion is a wonderful thing. No one tries to get pregnant just so they can terminate it. Even though it's not murder, it still eliminates a potential person, a potential daughter, a potential son. It's hard enough as it is. Women certainly don't need others telling them it's a murder.

It's not. On the contrary, abortion is an absolutely moral choice for any woman wishing to control her body.

Human Personhood Begins in the First Weeks of Pregnancy

Maureen L. Condic

Maureen L. Condic is an assistant professor of neurobiology and anatomy at the University of Utah and has conducted research on the regeneration of embryonic and adult neurons following spinal cord injury.

Legal and social arguments about when life begins are subjective and impossible to reconcile. However, the definition of death is scientific and objective: Death occurs when living cells cease to function in a coordinated manner for the continued maintenance of the body as a whole. This definition can be used to provide new insight on when human personhood begins. In the first weeks of pregnancy, human embryos develop the ability to act as an integrated whole—since this is the defining characteristic of life, embryos are living human organisms. Because embryos are living human beings, they should have the legal rights and protections associated with human personhood.

What defines the beginning of human life? This question has been the topic of considerable legal and social debate over the years since the Supreme Court's *Roe v. Wade* decision—debate that has only been intensified by the recent controversies over human embryonic stem cells and human cloning. Answers to this question run the full gamut from those who argue that life begins at conception (the view of more than one major world religion) to those arguing that babies are not to be considered fully human until a month after birth (the position of Princeton Professor of Bioethics Peter Singer).

The range of dissent and disagreement on the question of when human life begins has led many to believe it cannot be reasonably resolved in a pluralistic society. Courts have ruled that the diversity of opinion on the topic precludes a judicial resolution, requiring instead that the matter be addressed in the political arena, where accommodation of divergent views can be wrought through debate and compromise. Many Americans appear equally unwilling to impose a single interpretation on society, preferring instead to allow decisions regarding the beginning of life to be largely a matter of personal choice.

A Matter of Life and Death

While reluctance to impose a personal view on others is deeply ingrained in American society, one must question the legitimacy of such reluctance when the topic of our "imposition" is a matter (quite literally) of life and death. Few beyond the irrationally obdurate would maintain that human embryos are anything other than biologically *Homo sapiens* and alive, even at the earliest developmental stages. Equally few would contest the fact that, at early stages of embryonic development, human embryos bear little resemblance to anything we easily identify as "human." For most people, reconciling these two facts involves the uncomfortably fuzzy process of drawing a line somewhere during the continuously changing process of human prenatal development and asserting: "There. That's when human life begins—at least for me." It is precisely the subjectivity and inaccuracy of this decision that fuels our discomfort at "imposing" it on others.

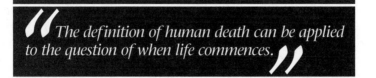

The definition of human death can be applied to the question of when life commences.

In contrast to the widespread disagreement over when human life begins, there is a broad social and legal consensus regarding when human life ends. Rarely has the point been made that the definition of human death can be applied to the question of when life commences with compelling symmetry. The definition of when life ends is both scientific and objective, and does not depend on personal belief or moral viewpoint. The current medical and legal understanding of death unambiguously defines both when human life ends and when it begins in a manner that is widely accepted and consistent with the legal and moral status of human beings at all stages of life. . . .

What does the nature of death tell us about the nature of human life? The medical and legal definition of death draws a clear distinction between living cells and living organisms. Organisms are living beings composed of parts that have separate but mutually dependent functions. While organisms are made of living cells, living cells themselves do not necessarily constitute an organism. The critical difference between a collection of cells and a living organism is the ability of an organism to act in a coordinated manner for the continued health and maintenance of the body as a whole. It is precisely this ability that breaks down at the moment of death, however death might occur. Dead bodies may have plenty of live cells, but their cells no longer function together in a coordinated manner. We can take living organs and cells from dead people for transplant to patients without a breach of ethics precisely because corpses are no longer living human beings. Human life is defined by the ability to function as an integrated whole—not by the mere presence of living human cells.

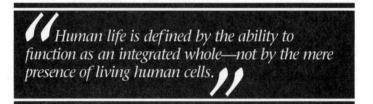

Human life is defined by the ability to function as an integrated whole—not by the mere presence of living human cells.

What does the nature of death tell us about the beginning of human life? From the earliest stages of development, human embryos clearly function as organisms. Embryos are not merely collections of human cells, but living creatures with all the properties that define any organism as distinct from a group of cells; embryos are capable of growing, maturing, maintaining a physiologic balance between various organ systems, adapting to changing circumstances and repairing injury. Mere groups of human cells do nothing like this under any circumstances. The embryo generates and organizes distinct tissues that function in a coordinated manner to maintain the continued growth and health of the developing body. Even within the fertilized egg itself there are distinct "parts" that must work together—specialized regions of cytoplasm that will give rise to unique derivatives once the fertilized egg divides into separate cells. Embryos are in full possession of the very characteristic that distinguishes a living human being from a dead one: the ability of all cells in the body to function together as an organism, with all parts acting in an integrated manner for the continued life and health of the body as a whole.

> *Embryos are in full possession of the very characteristic that distinguishes a living human being from a dead one: the ability of all cells in the body to function together as an organism.*

Linking human status to the nature of developing embryos is neither subjective nor open to personal opinion. Human embryos are living human beings precisely because they possess the single defining feature of human life that is lost in the moment of death—the ability to function as a coordinated organism rather than merely as a group of living human cells.

Other Definitions Are Subjective

What are the advantages of defining the beginning of human life in the same manner that we define its end, based on the integrated organismal function of human beings? To address this question, the alternative arguments regarding when life begins must be briefly considered. While at first inspection, there appear to be many divergent opinions regarding when human life commences, the common arguments are only of three general types: arguments from form, arguments from ability, and arguments from preference. The subjective and arbitrary nature of these arguments stands in stark contrast to the objective and unambiguous definition that organismal function provides for both the beginning and end of human life.

Of all the arguments regarding when human life begins, the most basic, and perhaps most intuitive, is that to be human, one must look human. Early human embryos are often described as "merely a ball of cells," and for many, it is difficult to imagine that something that looks more like a bag of marbles than a baby could possibly be a human being. Fundamentally, this argument asserts that human life is worthy of respect depending on appearance. When plainly stated, this conclusion is quite disturbing and also quite problematic. What level of malformation are we willing to accept before we revoke the right to continued existence? How are we to view children whose mature form will not be completely manifest until puberty? Form alone is a profoundly trivial and capricious basis for assigning human worth, and one that cannot be applied without considerable and obvious injustice.

> **A definition based on the organismal nature of human beings acknowledges that individuals with differing appearance, ability, and 'desirability' are, nonetheless, equally human.**

The superficiality of equating worth with form is sufficient for most to reject this argument and retreat to a functional definition: form per se is not the issue; rather, it is the ability to function as a human being that defines the beginning of human life. Human beings are capable of a number of distinctive functions (self-awareness, reason, language, and so forth) that are acquired gradually over prenatal life as development proceeds. Therefore, the argument goes, human worth is also gradually acquired, with early embryos being less human than more developed fetuses.

Other Definitions Lead to Problematic Conclusions

A number of seemingly independent arguments regarding when life begins are in fact variations on this argument from ability. Thus, the proposal that human life begins when the fetus becomes "viable," or capable of surviving outside of the womb, is a subset of the ability argument that gives conclusive weight to the suite of abilities required for survival independent of the mother. Similarly, the common argument that embryos are human when they are in the womb of the mother (where they can develop into babies), while embryos generated in the laboratory are not, is also a variation on the ability argument that equates developmental ability with human life and worth.

While the argument from ability is less superficial than the argument from form alone, it is no less problematic. As noted above, functional definitions have been repeatedly rejected as a legal basis for the definition of death, in part due to their arbitrary nature. One can certainly identify any number of elderly and disabled people who are less functionally adept than newborn infants—and perhaps even late-term fetuses. While Western culture has a strong tradition of meritocracy, providing greater economic and social rewards to those who demonstrate greater achievement, basic human rights are not meted out according to performance. Unless we are willing to assign "personhood" proportionate to ability (young children, for example, might be only 20 percent human, while people with myopia 95 percent), the limited abilities of prenatal humans are irrelevant to their status as human beings.

> *Embryos are genetically unique human organisms, fully possessing the integrated biologic function that defines human life.*

The final and perhaps the most emotionally compelling argument for assigning human status to a developing embryo is the extent to which parents desire a child. Yet the argument from being wanted, which equates status as a human being with the desire of a second party who has the power to confer or deny that status, essentially reduces the definition of a human being to a matter of preference. You are human because I choose to view you that way. The fact that human status can be positively conferred for "wanted" embryos as well as denied for the "unwanted" illustrates the fundamental arbitrariness of this argument. The preferences of individuals who possess the power to impose them on others are hardly a compelling basis for legislation on human life.

Despite the apparent diversity of views regarding when human life begins, the common arguments thus reduce to three general classes (form, ability, and preference), all of which are highy subjective and impossible to reconcile with our current legal and moral view of postnatal human worth. It is, in fact, the subjectivity and inconsistency of these views, rather than their diversity, that makes them so unsatisfying as a basis for legislation on human life.

An Objective Definition Is Necessary

Unlike other definitions, understanding human life to be an intrinsic property of human organisms does not require subjective judgments regarding "quality of life" or relative worth. A definition based on the organismal nature of human beings acknowledges that individuals with differing appearance, ability, and "desirability" are, nonetheless, equally human. It is precisely the objective nature of such a definition (compared to vague "quality of life" assessments) that has made organismal function so compelling a basis for the legal definition of death.

Once the nature of human beings as organisms has been abandoned as the basis for assigning legal personhood, it is difficult to propose an alternative definition that could not be used to deny humanity to virtually anyone. Arguments that deny human status to embryos based on form, ability, or choice can be readily turned against adult humans who have imperfect form, limited ability, or who simply constitute an inconvenience to more powerful individuals or groups. Indeed, such arguments can be quite protean in their ability to deny rights to anyone not meeting an arbitrary criterion for humanity. Abraham Lincoln made this very point regarding arguments based on form, ability, and choice that were put forth in his day to justify the institution of slavery:

> It is color, then; the lighter having the right to enslave the darker? Take care. By this rule, you are to be slave to the first man you meet with a fairer skin than your own.
>
> You do not mean color exactly? You mean the whites are intellectually the superiors of the blacks, and, therefore, have the right to enslave them? Take care again. By this rule, you are to be slave to the first man you meet with an intellect superior to your own.
>
> But, say you, it is a question of interest; and, if you

can make it your interest, you have the right to enslave another. Very well. And if he can make it his
interest, he has the right to enslave you. . . .

Prenatal Life Is Human Life

Embryos are genetically unique human organisms, fully possessing the integrated biologic function that defines human life
at all stages of development, continuing throughout adulthood
until death. The ability to act as an integrated whole is the only
function that departs from our bodies in the moment of death,
and is therefore the defining characteristic of "human life."
This definition does not depend on religious belief or subjective judgment. From the landmark case of Karen Ann Quinlan
(1976) on, the courts have consistently upheld organismal
function as the legal definition of human life. Failure to apply
the same standard that so clearly defines the end of human life
to its beginning is both inconsistent and unwarranted.

The conclusion that human life is defined by integrated (organismal) function has wide-reaching implications, both political and moral. While the public domain has limited authority to
promote morality, it does have both the power and the responsibility to prevent harm to individuals. A consistent definition of
what constitutes human life, both at its beginning and at its end,
requires that current legislation dealing with prenatal human
life be considered in light of both biological fact and accepted legal precedent regarding the definition of human life. If current
legislation enables and supports the killing of human beings
based on a scientifically flawed understanding of human life,
laws can and should be revised. Clearly, such a revision would
not be without political cost. Yet allowing life-or-death decisions
to be based on arbitrary or capricious definitions is also a course
of action that is not without considerable social and moral cost.

6

Human Personhood Begins at Birth

William Westmiller

William Westmiller is the chairman of the Republican Liberty Caucus and cofounder of the Canadian Libertarian Party. His commentaries on political issues have been published on several major Internet Web sites.

The definition of a "person" is critical to the debate on abortion because every person has a right to life. The one characteristic that separates a human being from all other living things, such as skin cells or trees, is the capacity to reason. Because an embryo or a fetus does not achieve the independent capacity for rational thought until actual birth, personhood is not fully realized until birth.

The Declaration of Independence asserts, and fundamental libertarian principles recognize, that every person has a right to his or her own life, liberty and pursuit of happiness, provided they do not infringe on the equal rights of another person.

In this context, "rights" are proper claims to what is naturally due a person. A "person" is a human being. Not a human might-be, or a human used-to-be, but a homo-sapien with the capacity to reason. This definition of "person" is critical to the defense of individual rights.

We all know the difference between a person and a dog, a tree or a rock. But modern technology has shown us pictures of the fetus in utero and it becomes even more personal with the use of ultrasound in nearly every pregnancy. A late term fetus looks very much like a real baby. But it isn't.

Personhood Is Defined
by the Capacity to Reason

A person is a living human. So is a fetus. But, so is any other cell on our bodies. In fact, modern genetics inform us that every cell that contains human DNA has all the potential required to develop into a complete person. Even a dead skin cell, like a dandruff flake, has all the genetic potential, given the proper environment, to become a person. So, we can't use "human" or "living" as definitive characteristics of a person. There is only one characteristic that is unique to human beings and distinguishes every person from any other living thing. That is the capacity to reason.

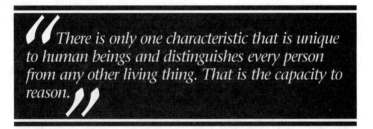

There is only one characteristic that is unique to human beings and distinguishes every person from any other living thing. That is the capacity to reason.

In the known universe, only a *person* has the capacity to form abstract concepts from complex perceptions, apply logic to those concepts, test them against the memory of other concepts, form unique and creative ideas, and communicate those ideas to others. If you recognize any of these activities, the odds are very high that you are a person.

Of course, there can be no ability to reason without the physical structures and biologic functions that make it possible. Brain development and operative sensory organs allow any animal to attain consciousness, but that is not a unique human quality. It is not sufficient for a being to simply have physical resources, it also requires the ability to use them. The capacity to reason has many predicates, but the actual capacity only comes to fruition at birth. . . .

Personhood Exists Despite Impaired Capacity

There is a difference between having a capacity and the exercise of that capacity. Any person's ability to reason may be impaired, neglected or evaded, without actually losing the capacity for rational thought. Capacity either exists or it does not. It is a qualitative, not a quantitative, characteristic of persons. Once acquired, the capacity persists and is presumed to remain until it is proven by objective facts that the capacity has been lost forever. Death will do that to you. Sleep won't.

Guardian rights can be derived only from the natural rights of a person.

The amount of intellectual ability or the quantity of rational capacity is only relevant when it comes to the legal question of whether a person requires a guardian for the protection of their natural rights. A person may be dependent on another for nourishment and sustenance. The guardian—usually the natural parents—assumes the responsibility for the defense of a child's natural rights. That circumstance can also apply to retarded, aged, infirm or otherwise handicapped adults. None of these physical impediments compromise the personhood of the debilitated.

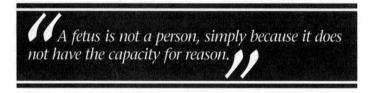

A fetus is not a person, simply because it does not have the capacity for reason.

There are many deformities, injuries, and diseases—short of death—which may eliminate any capacity for reason. A persistent and irreversible vegetative state is not the human condition. The burdens of a guardian are not to be envied and the law should clearly articulate the presumptions that should apply to any guardian's exercise of a dependent's rights. But government cannot assume guardianship of a being that is not a person and thereby violate a woman's natural rights to control her own life.

A Potential Person Is Not a Person

A potential is the total absence of an essential attribute.

The distinction between capacity and potential is critical. Capacity is a real ability, while potential is the mere possibility. Since we are all potentially dead, we cannot base individual rights on a mere potential. In the same sense, we cannot base rights on the premise that a zygote, embryo or fetus has the potential to become something different. It is not an "unborn baby" or a "preborn child", it is what it is.

A fetus is not a person, simply because it does not have the capacity for reason. For most of its development, it isn't even viable: it can't survive outside the womb. Until very late in gestation, the fetus lacks the neural capacity to even process basic animal sensations. At the verge of birth, a fetus with a fully developed brain still lacks the complex sensory input that makes the potential for reasoning a reality. It is no more rational than any other fully developed mammal.

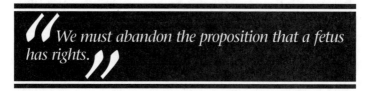

We must abandon the proposition that a fetus has rights.

Human birth is a seminal event: everything changes. The potential for distinctly human acts is realized, and the fetus gains the independent capacity for rational thought, becoming an individual. A child has (hopefully) come to "term" and developed all the physical capacity for "independent" survival; it is no longer a "parasitic" part of the mother, it begins to independently breath its own oxygen; it is exposed for the first time to complex sensory stimulation; the brain begins to distinguish, process, and recall the perceptions of reality which are beyond its own existence; the child acquires the raw sensory materials for integration, abstraction and formation of concepts. The manipulation of these concepts—reason—is now within its mental capacity. The potential for human personhood is fully realized at birth.

A Fetus Does Not Have Rights

Rights are proper claims.

Any assertion we make to ownership is a claim. Whether it is a just and proper claim depends on the nature of the claim and the thing being claimed. When we claim a right to our life, we make an assertion of sole ownership. No other person can claim to own, possess, or terminate our life. There is only one person, one life, which cannot be divided, compromised nor infringed without a violation of that basic right. All other rights derive from this basic right to life. . . .

All rights are individual rights because every person is an individual. There are no such thing as "group rights" or "state rights" that conflict with individual rights. Nor is there any such thing as "fetal rights" that conflict with any real person's rights.

Rights do not conflict. They are always complementary expressions of the proper claims of every individual. Natural rights are inextricably—inalienably—vested in the person who possesses them. They cannot be extracted, transferred or sold to another at any price.

Even if we were to grant—beyond all reason—the right of a fetus to life, we could not deny or infringe the self-evident right of a woman to her own life. Nevertheless, that is what many "pro-choice" proponents suggest.

Courts incline toward the historic autonomy concepts of Anglo-American law, attempting to predict the possibility of independent physical survival. Asserting "viability" as grounds for a claim of rights is not just vague (16–24 weeks of gestation), but elevates physical attributes above unique human characteristics. Biologists go a step further, drawing a slightly less vague line (7–9 weeks) where unique physical traits of homo-sapiens are evident. Many theologic advocates suggest an earlier line (1–2 weeks) when the fertilized human zygote is implanted in the uterus and becomes an embryo.

All of these proponents focus on physical characteristics which might identify a human, rather than the mental characteristics that distinguish a human person. They all grant the state a right to conscript the woman's body on behalf of an embryo or fetus that barely has the potential to become a person. They all lead to preposterous legal contradictions and perilous consequences for every woman.

Unless we are prepared to grant rights to bacteria, monkeys and trees; unless we are willing to prosecute women for capital crimes, we must abandon the proposition that a fetus has rights. The fetus is a part of the woman until birth and every woman has every right to terminate her own pregnancy whenever she pleases. That choice should be thoughtfully considered, in the absence of any government subsidy or penalty.

7

Women Should Have Access to the Abortion Pill RU-486

S. Boyd

S. Boyd is a medical editor and freelance writer.

The right to choose abortion is a serious responsibility and requires soul-searching and awareness. The ability to take control over one's body and make critical decisions that affect it can bring a high sense of empowerment and self-esteem. These decisions include which method to use for terminating a pregnancy, whether it be surgical abortion or the use of mifepristone, commonly known as RU-486. RU-486 has been shown to be safe and effective, and it should be made available to all women.

Editor's note: The following viewpoint was originally published on September 18, 2000. On September 28, 2000, the Food and Drug Administration approved mifepristone for use in the United States.

"How do you feel?"

The nurse prepares to capture my answer, her pen poised over a sheaf of response forms. I hesitate, a little afraid to answer truthfully. But this was a study. How were other women going to know what they were missing if I withheld the truth?

"I feel . . . empowered."

Now it was the nurse's turn to hesitate. "Empowered? How so? Could you explain that?"

How could I explain how much the abortion had changed me? An unwanted pregnancy is terrifying, paralyzing. When the line appeared on that urine-soaked stick my life came to a standstill. My body was a strange vessel, harboring something that threatened to sabotage the rest of my life.

The Dilemma of Unwanted Pregnancy

My initial reaction was denial, followed by a desire for the whole situation—the pregnancy, the doctor's visit, the difficult choice ahead—to go away. If I wanted to regain control of my body, I needed to terminate this pregnancy. But in order to do that, I would have to relinquish control and endure what I understood to be my only option: invasive surgery performed by a stranger. Under the circumstances, I wanted the ordeal finished immediately.

Making the decision to terminate a pregnancy or to bring a fetus to term is by far the most wrenching experience I've ever had. The right to choose is not a luxury; it is a responsibility that demands intense introspection and awareness. It is frequently suggested that abortion itself causes undue psychological strain, exhibited by depression, nightmares and feelings of loss and regret. In fact, most of those symptoms come from the process of discovering an unwanted pregnancy and choosing what to do about it.

My abortion counselor was very supportive. She listened patiently to my tight, teary voice. Somehow, in the midst of all my questions and worries, she managed to tell me about a procedure that didn't involve surgery. It could be done immediately, not at the seven-week point, which was two weeks away. I could avoid all the invasive metal instruments. I could do it at home, where I would be in charge of my level of comfort, privacy and activity.

She offered me RU-486.

How RU-486 Works

The safety and efficacy of RU-486 (mifepristone) as an abortifacient have been documented in France for almost 20 years and in the U.S.—for research only—since 1996. In most American studies, mifepristone is administered orally in the doctor's office. The drug works to block the production of progesterone, a hormone that is necessary for the maintenance of pregnancy.

(Progesterone facilitates the embedding of a fertilized egg in the uterine walls and suppresses the uterine contractions associated with menstruation.) A second medication involved in a medical abortion, misoprostol or Cytotec, is taken at least 24 hours after mifepristone. Misoprostol induces contractions, allowing a "miscarriage" to occur. . . .

I became one of the thousands of women to participate in the preapproval studies of RU-486. On the day of my appointment I sat on the examining table, fully dressed. The nurse handed me the pill along with a paper cup of water. "After you take this pill there is no backing out."

I nodded. I felt like I held my future in the palm of my hand—one little white pill, no bigger than a tablet of aspirin. I swallowed and that was it. I received a packet of the vaginal tablets and a final reminder about appropriate misoprostol use, and I was on my way. On the drive home, I imagined I could feel the progesterone decreasing throughout my body.

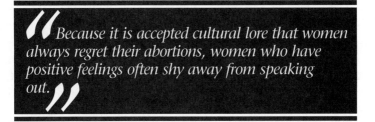

Because it is accepted cultural lore that women always regret their abortions, women who have positive feelings often shy away from speaking out.

In several mifepristone/misoprostol trials, including mine, women were allowed to administer the misoprostol themselves, in the privacy of their own homes, allowing them full control over the experience. The at-home procedure was relatively easy. There were cramps, the pain stifled by regular doses of ibuprofen. Bleeding began within half an hour. I lay in my own bed, my husband in the next room. Expulsion of the fetal tissue takes four hours or more—a slow pace I welcomed after the panicky weeks that came before. For the first time since my positive pregnancy test I began to regain control over my body and my anxiety.

A Sense of Empowerment

For weeks after the abortion I would turn to my husband at random moments to say, "I know this is strange, but I feel like the abortion was a good experience." I felt so strong. Unwanted pregnancy is something that every sexually active woman fears. I had faced that fear and, in the process, reached deep within myself to evaluate my beliefs, my priorities and the value of life. I didn't expect such strength to emerge after the abortion. Wasn't I supposed to be anxious and filled with regret?

I was surprised to learn that feelings of increased self-esteem and well-being after an abortion are not uncommon. Not only is abortion a psychologically benign procedure, but women who have had one abortion have higher overall self-esteem than women who bring an unwanted pregnancy to term, according to a 1992 study published in the journal *Professional Psychology*.

A 1989 study published in *Family Planning Perspectives* even controlled for self-esteem, dividing women into three groups at the time of their pregnancy test: not pregnant; pregnant and had a child; and pregnant and had an abortion. There were few initial differences between the women, but during follow-up it was found that women in the abortion group scored significantly higher on self-esteem.

Though only a minority of women, usually those who are predisposed to depression, report feelings of loss and emotional turmoil after abortion, negative psychological effects are often considered the norm. Information about "post-abortion stress syndrome," a condition whose existence is not recognized by the American Psychological Association or the American Psychiatric Association, is readily available to women who have negative post-abortion feelings. Positive feedback, however, is often lacking.

Because it is accepted cultural lore that women always regret their abortions, women who have positive feelings often shy away from speaking out. Though it is a legal choice, abortion still is stigmatized as a "necessary evil."

Medical Abortion Is About Choice

Conflicting political, religious and personal views about abortion have clouded the debate about the use of RU-486. Medical abortion is not about legality or morality. It *is* about choice—but not the choice of whether to end an unwanted pregnancy. Instead, it is an option for the *method* of terminating a pregnancy. Why should a woman's right to choose end once she has decided to get an abortion? Is it fair to limit the ways she can take advantage of a basic right?

According to a report published in the *Journal of the American Medical Women's Association*, women of various races, ethnicities, education levels and socioeconomic backgrounds in the United States have reported their satisfaction with the mifepristone-misoprostol medical abortion. The primary appeal of medical abortion appears to be the option of aborting at home.

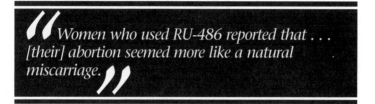

Women who used RU-486 reported that . . . [their] abortion seemed more like a natural miscarriage.

Besides avoiding invasive surgery, women who used RU-486 reported that the medical abortion seemed more like a natural miscarriage, even though they understood it was produced by a pharmaceutical. They benefited from having a partner or friend with them during the abortion, something that is not allowed at most abortion clinics; and medical abortion counselors spend twice as much time with women as do the counselors for surgical abortion, giving women more time to ask questions and further solidify their abortion decision. As one study participant stated, "The fact that you insert [misoprostol] yourself is a feeling like . . . this is my choice . . . my decision. There's so much more power in it."

RU-486 made my abortion experience less stressful, almost enjoyable. I was not required to lie undressed while a doctor probed and poked inside of me. I took a pill; I terminated the pregnancy; I spent the afternoon with my body, in the privacy of my own home, regaining power. There was no one else I could blame for the outcome, but more important, there was no one else who could take credit for my new strength. . . .

The studies on RU-486 completed thus far have opened the door to private, individualized reproductive control for thousands of women. There is no reason why all women, regardless of their feelings about unwanted pregnancy, shouldn't have every option available to increase control over their fertility—and their lives.

8

The Abortion Pill RU-486 Should Be Banned

Gregory Rummo

Gregory Rummo is a conservative Christian columnist.

When the Food and Drug Administration deemed the abortion pill RU-486 as safe and effective, it approved a drug that destroys the lives of unborn children. Furthermore, it may not be safe for the mother, as numerous complications, even death, have been cited after its use. Human life is sacred, including life that is inside a mother's womb. The approval of RU-486 should be withdrawn.

RU-486 was approved by the Food and Drug Administration in September [2000]. The FDA approves a pharmaceutical after many years of scrutiny in the laboratory and in clinical trials where the drug is tested for safety and efficacy in humans. When the FDA reviewers are satisfied, the drug is "proved" and deemed as "safe and effective."

But something odd happened with the approval of RU-486. This was the first time this government regulatory body, which oversees the safety of the nation's food and pharmaceuticals, approved a drug meant not to preserve a life but to destroy another human being as though it were an infectious disease or parasite.

It seems that the FDA has forgotten the Hippocratic Oath, an ancient code of ethics followed by physicians. The oath stipulates, in part: "I will give no deadly medicine to anyone if asked, nor suggest any such counsel; and in like manner I will not give to a woman a pessary to produce abortion."

RU-486 Is Not Safe

And safety? That's an interesting matter for debate. The drug is certainly not safe to the developing life inside the mother's uterus. The FDA has approved a deadly poison and declared it "safe."

On top of this, there are lingering questions about the drug's safety to the woman—despite what you may have heard to the contrary. Abortion proponents have touted RU-486 as a simple method for ending pregnancy.

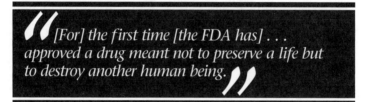

[For] the first time [the FDA has] . . . approved a drug meant not to preserve a life but to destroy another human being.

On the surface, this would appear to be true—what could be easier than popping a pill? Even the copy for the ads—"You have the freedom to choose, and now you have another safe abortion choice," along with the picture of the "crisply dressed woman gazing out a window"—all seem to imply safety and simplicity.

But this is hardly the case.

RU-486 Is Deadly

Women have been sold a bill of goods. A chemical abortion using RU-486 is not simple. It's not just one pill, and there may be numerous complications and side effects. There also have been some deaths of women reported during the testing of the regimen.

Dr. George Grant, author of the book "The Legacy of Planned Parenthood," has characterized RU-486 as "horrific" in a recent radio interview on "Focus on the Family." Grant dispelled the myths about RU-486 being uncomplicated, safe, and pain-free.

"It is portrayed as a miracle," he said. But a chemical abortion performed with RU-486 is "much more painful, requires a longer period of treatment, more office visits, and has longer-term effects than any of the current surgical abortion procedures," he said. One of the side effects mentioned by Grant is a 70-day menses (period) following an abortion using RU-486.

A chemical abortion using RU-486 is really a regimen of at least two drugs. Mifepristone, sold under the brand name Mifeprex, blocks the effects of progesterone and thus ends the life of the developing infant. A second drug, misoprostal, is typically used to induce labor. But in the case of abortion, it promotes the expulsion of the dead infant; it is required as part of a supervised regimen including three visits to the abortion practitioner's office.

But the bad news doesn't end with complications and potential side effects.

There also have been reports of women who have died from an RU-486 abortion. "The number of women who have died in the testing of RU-486 ought to create astonishment," Grant said. "Nine in France, 18 in Italy died—most of them from cardiac arrest."

Grant believes the FDA has made a mistake approving RU-486 and he believes that its approval will ultimately be withdrawn.

Human Life Is Sacred

"People are made in the image of God," Grant explains, "and therefore, there is a sanctity attached to human life."

God has declared the creation and development of a human life as sacred. The author of Psalm 139 praises God for his intimate knowledge of every human life—from its very beginning. "O Lord, you have searched me and you know me. . . . For you created my inmost being; you knit me together in my mother's womb."

When humans try to impose their destructive ways on this process, there will always be unexpected complications and consequences.

The Bible warns in Galatians 6:7: "Do not be deceived. God cannot be mocked. A man reaps what he sows."

Now there's a warning you won't see in any of those magazine ads.

9

Partial-Birth Abortion Is Ethical

Rob Deters

Rob Deters is a law student at the University of Wisconsin.

"Partial-birth abortion" is the name that anti-abortionists have given to a procedure known as intact dilation and extraction, in which, sixteen weeks into pregnancy, a nonviable fetus is removed from a woman's uterus. Anti-abortionists emphasize that the fetus's skull is collapsed in this procedure, so that it can pass through the woman's undilated cervix. The details of the procedure make many people uncomfortable, but the fact is that all abortions involve the destruction of the fetus—to single out a single type of abortion procedure is arbitrary. The fetus is not a person, and a woman should have the right to abort it, through whatever procedure a doctor recommends.

Editor's note: The following viewpoint was written in October 2003. In November 2003, President George W. Bush signed into law the Partial Birth Abortion Ban Act, which prohibits abortion procedures in which a living fetus is intentionally killed while partly or completely outside the body of the mother.

Let's be clear. Abortion is not murder. If it were, the Supreme Court would not uphold it as constitutional. If it were, the American Medical Association, whose opinion on health and ethics I hold in high esteem, wouldn't support abortion as a viable medical procedure. Abortion is murder only if you choose to define it as such, but there is no such definition that you can make every rational person believe.

All Abortions Destroy the Fetus

Partial-birth abortion, or, more accurately, intact dilation and extraction, is a technique by which a non-viable fetus is removed from a woman's uterus. The skull of the fetus is collapsed via a cervical incision and suction rather than crushed with forceps.

The other technique used at this stage in a woman's pregnancy is dilation and evacuation, which calls for the dismemberment of the body of the fetus with forceps and its removal from the uterus.

No law to ban "partial-birth abortions" prohibits this second procedure, just the first.

All abortions are performed with the end result being the destruction of a fetus; it's simply the method that we're discussing. You can scrape, suck, crush or surgically remove fetal tissue from a woman all for the same purpose—to terminate a pregnancy.

Why does this technique even exist? Dilation and extraction is simply an option for a doctor to use when a woman is at a very specific point in her pregnancy. At 16 weeks into a pregnancy, a fetal skull is too large to pass through a non-dilated cervix. At 17 weeks, the bones in a fetus begin to calcify, leading to a higher probability of injury to a woman's uterus because of bony fragments.

These two techniques are options for a doctor to choose from in order to perform the abortion in the safest way possible. At 24 weeks (the end of the second trimester) abortions are outlawed as a voluntary procedure and are only performed if there is a medical emergency.

Bans Are Unconstitutional

The argument over dilation and extraction is all about politics, not about a woman's health. There are no studies that show dilation and extraction is a more dangerous procedure or that it leads to problems getting pregnant in the future. In fact, many doctors feel the procedure has many benefits, including fewer instruments used in the uterus, less chance of infection and shorter operating time.

Squeamish yet? Of course you are. That's exactly how conservatives want you to feel. They want to use the natural reaction we have to this medical procedure (feeling uncomfortable) to make an argument that just doesn't hold. In fact, it doesn't hold in courts of law very much at all.

Previous attempts to limit dilation and extraction have all been struck down. [In 2000] the Supreme Court in *Stenberg vs. Carhart* ruled that Nebraska's ban on dilation and extraction was unconstitutional. It cited two reasons: there was no exception for the woman's health, and the ban placed an "undue burden" on the woman's right to choose. Although it was a close call (a 5-4 vote), it still didn't pass muster.

The current law being discussed in conference committee at the Capitol in Washington, D.C., is little different.

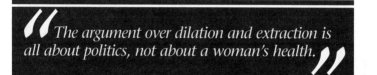

The argument over dilation and extraction is all about politics, not about a woman's health.

Many opponents of the "partial-birth abortion" ban that just passed both the House and the Senate (it's simply being revised) say it will take just a matter of time until the Supreme Court strikes it down just like it did Nebraska's law. This is probably true, but the narrow margin of the previous decision doesn't make this an absolute.

[Editor's note: As of December 2004, the Supreme Court had not reviewed the Partial Birth Abortion Ban Act.]

Government Intrusion

What is really going on here is far more pernicious. "Partial-birth abortion" is a scare campaign. It's a way for conservatives to pounce on a tiny fact, blow it up out of proportion and make political hay.

If dilation and extraction is so terrible and we have to limit it by law, it must be rampant, right? Wrong. In 1996, the last year for which statistics are available, there were 1.4 million abortions performed in this country. Of them, only 650 were "partial-birth abortions."　·

Conservatives believe that a government that governs the least governs the best. For conservatives, when it comes to morality, a government that is the most intrusive is the ideal.

Currently, many of this nation's conservatives are demanding abstinence-only sex education, taking stands against the decriminalization of drugs and legislating that marriage be defined by law as between a man and a woman. This is fundamentalism at its most obvious. Conservatives—Republicans or not—demand your lifestyle, your choices and your options be limited to those with which they themselves feel comfortable.

A woman's right to choose is based on a simple premise: A fetus is not a person until it can live outside the womb. Until that point, it is up to the woman, for health, personal, economic or social reasons, to either carry to term or terminate that pregnancy. There is no "child" and there is no "person"—there is a thing.

10

Partial-Birth Abortion Is Unethical and Should Be Banned

U.S. Congress

The Congress forms the legislative body of the U.S. government. The following viewpoint is excerpted from the Partial Birth Abortion Ban Act, which was passed by the 108th Congress and became law in November 2003. It prohibits abortion procedures in which a living fetus is intentionally killed while partly or completely outside the body of the mother.

Congress passed the Partial Birth Abortion Ban Act of 2003 because the procedure is morally, medically, and ethically inhumane. No medical evidence exists that a partial-birth abortion is ever necessary to preserve the health of a woman; in fact, the procedure actually poses severe risks for women. Partial-birth abortions are ethically different from other abortions because the fetus is killed outside the womb and fully experiences the pain involved.

The Congress finds and declares the following:

(1) A moral, medical, and ethical consensus exists that the practice of performing a partial-birth abortion—an abortion in which a physician delivers an unborn child's body until only the head remains inside the womb, punctures the back of the child's skull with a sharp instrument, and sucks the child's brains out before completing delivery of the dead infant—is a gruesome and inhumane procedure that is never medically

The 108th Congress of the United States of America, "Partial Birth Abortion Ban Act of 2003," 2003.

necessary and should be prohibited.

(2) Rather than being an abortion procedure that is embraced by the medical community, particularly among physicians who routinely perform other abortion procedures, partial-birth abortion remains a disfavored procedure that is not only unnecessary to preserve the health of the mother, but in fact poses serious risks to the long-term health of women and in some circumstances, their lives. As a result, at least 27 States banned the procedure as did the United States Congress which voted to ban the procedure during the 104th, 105th, and 106th Congresses. . . .

The Mother's Health

(13) There exists substantial record evidence upon which Congress has reached its conclusion that a ban on partial-birth abortion is not required to contain a "health" exception, because the facts indicate that a partial-birth abortion is never necessary to preserve the health of a woman, poses serious risks to a woman's health, and lies outside the standard of medical care. Congress was informed by extensive hearings held during the 104th, 105th, and 107th Congresses and passed a ban on partial-birth abortion in the 104th, 105th, and 106th Congresses. These findings reflect the very informed judgment of the Congress that a partial-birth abortion is never necessary to preserve the health of a woman, poses serious risks to a woman's health, and lies outside the standard of medical care, and should, therefore, be banned.

(13) (14) Pursuant to the testimony received during extensive legislative hearings during the 104th, 105th, and 107th Congresses, Congress finds and declares that:

> *Partial-birth abortion poses serious risks to the health of a woman undergoing the procedure.*

(A) Partial-birth abortion poses serious risks to the health of a woman undergoing the procedure. Those risks include, among other things: an increase in a woman's risk of suffering from cervical incompetence, a result of cervical dilation making it difficult or impossible for a woman to successfully carry a subsequent pregnancy to term; an increased risk of uterine rupture, abruption, amniotic fluid embolus, and trauma to the uterus as a result of converting the child to a footling breech position, a procedure which, according to a leading obstetrics textbook, "there are very few, if any, indications for . . . other than for delivery of a second twin"; and a risk of lacerations and secondary hemorrhaging due to the doctor blindly forcing a sharp instrument into the base of the unborn child's skull while he or she is lodged in the birth canal, an act which could result in severe bleeding, brings with it the threat of shock, and could ultimately result in maternal death.

Never Necessary

(B) There is no credible medical evidence that partial-birth abortions are safe or are safer than other abortion procedures. No controlled studies of partial-birth abortions have been conducted nor have any comparative studies been conducted to demonstrate its safety and efficacy compared to other abortion methods. Furthermore, there have been no articles published in peer-reviewed journals that establish that partial-birth abortions are superior in any way to established abortion procedures. Indeed, unlike other more commonly used abortion procedures, there are currently no medical schools that provide instruction on abortions that include the instruction in partial-birth abortions in their curriculum.

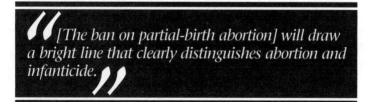

[The ban on partial-birth abortion] will draw a bright line that clearly distinguishes abortion and infanticide.

(C) A prominent medical association has concluded that partial-birth abortion is "not an accepted medical practice," that it has "never been subject to even a minimal amount of the normal medical practice development," that "the relative advantages and disadvantages of the procedure in specific circumstances remain unknown," and that "there is no consensus among obstetricians about its use". The association has further noted that partial-birth abortion is broadly disfavored by both medical experts and the public, is "ethically wrong," and "is never the only appropriate procedure.". . .

(E) The physician credited with developing the partial-birth abortion procedure has testified that he has never encountered a situation where a partial-birth abortion was medically necessary to achieve the desired outcome and, thus, is never medically necessary to preserve the health of a woman.

(F) A ban on the partial-birth abortion procedure will therefore advance the health interests of pregnant women seeking to terminate a pregnancy.

Respect for Human Life

(G) In light of this overwhelming evidence, Congress and the States have a compelling interest in prohibiting partial-birth abortions. In addition to promoting maternal health, such a prohibition will draw a bright line that clearly distinguishes abortion and infanticide, that preserves the integrity of the medical profession, and promotes respect for human life.

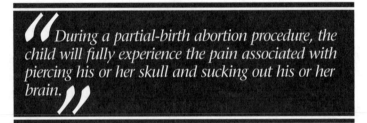

During a partial-birth abortion procedure, the child will fully experience the pain associated with piercing his or her skull and sucking out his or her brain.

(H) Based upon *Roe v. Wade* (410 U.S. 113 (1973)) and *Planned Parenthood v. Casey* (505 U.S. 833 (1992)), a governmental interest in protecting the life of a child during the delivery process arises by virtue of the fact that during a partial-birth abortion, labor is induced and the birth process has begun. This distinction was recognized in *Roe* when the Court noted, without comment, that the Texas parturition statute, which prohibited one from killing a child "in a state of being born and before actual birth," was not under attack. This interest becomes compelling as the child emerges from the maternal body. A child that is completely born is a full, legal person entitled to constitutional protections afforded a "person" under the United States Constitution. Partial-birth abortions involve the killing of a child that is in the process, in fact mere inches away from, becoming a "person". Thus, the government has a heightened interest in protecting the life of the partially-born child.

(I) This, too, has not gone unnoticed in the medical community, where a prominent medical association has recognized that partial-birth abortions are "ethically different from other destructive abortion techniques because the fetus, normally twenty weeks or longer in gestation, is killed outside of the womb". According to this medical association, the "'partial birth' gives the fetus an autonomy which separates it from the right of the woman to choose treatments for her own body".

(J) Partial-birth abortion also confuses the medical, legal, and ethical duties of physicians to preserve and promote life, as the physician acts directly against the physical life of a child, whom he or she had just delivered, all but the head, out of the womb, in order to end that life. Partial-birth abortion thus appropriates the terminology and techniques used by obstetricians in the delivery of living children—obstetricians who preserve and protect the life of the mother and the child and instead uses those techniques to end the life of the partially-born child.

(K) Thus, by aborting a child in the manner that purposefully seeks to kill the child after he or she has begun the process of birth, partial-birth abortion undermines the public's perception of the appropriate role of a physician during the delivery process, and perverts a process during which life is brought into the world, in order to destroy a partially-born child.

(L) The gruesome and inhumane nature of the partial-birth abortion procedure and its disturbing similarity to the killing of a newborn infant promotes a complete disregard for infant human life that can only be countered by a prohibition of the procedure.

Partial-Birth Abortions Are Inhumane

(M) The vast majority of babies killed during partial-birth abortions are alive until the end of the procedure. It is a medical fact, however, that unborn infants at this stage can feel pain when subjected to painful stimuli and that their perception of this pain is even more intense than that of newborn infants and older children when subjected to the same stimuli. Thus, during a partial-birth abortion procedure, the child will fully experience the pain associated with piercing his or her skull and sucking out his or her brain.

(N) Implicitly approving such a brutal and inhumane procedure by choosing not to prohibit it will further coarsen society to the humanity of not only newborns, but all vulnerable and innocent human life, making it increasingly difficult to protect such life. Thus, Congress has a compelling interest in acting—indeed it must act—to prohibit this inhumane procedure.

(O) For these reasons, Congress finds that partial-birth abortion is never medically indicated to preserve the health of the mother, is in fact unrecognized as a valid abortion procedure by the mainstream medical community; poses additional health risks to the mother; blurs the line between abortion and infanticide in the killing of a partially-born child just inches from birth; and confuses the role of the physician in childbirth and should, therefore, be banned.

11

The Ban on Partial-Birth Abortion Undermines Abortion Rights

Gloria Feldt

Gloria Feldt is the president of Planned Parenthood Federation of America, the largest provider and advocate of reproductive health care in the country. She is the author of The War on Choice, *from which the following viewpoint is excerpted.*

President George W. Bush signed into law the Partial Birth Abortion Ban Act on November 5, 2003, even though the Supreme Court had previously struck an identical law down as being unconstitutional. The Partial Birth Abortion Ban Act is part of a larger campaign to make all abortions illegal, and it attacks the reproductive rights that women have fought long and hard to obtain. Politicians should not be allowed to tell physicians or women what procedure to use for any surgery, including abortion.

On November 5, 2003, President George W. Bush took a giant step toward fulfilling his promise to restrict abortion. He signed a criminal ban on abortion procedures, the deceptively named "Partial Birth Abortion [Ban] Act." Surrounded by a phalanx of gray-haired, self-congratulatory white men—and no women!—he signed away a great portion of women's power over their reproductive lives. This was an ominous milestone: for the first time in history, the two houses of Congress had passed, and a president had signed into law, a federal law criminalizing established medical procedures. With the House of Representatives, the Senate, and the White House now aligned in lockstep, ready to take away women's reproductive rights, the right wing's war on women and choice had scored a major victory. . . .

This Ban Defies the Supreme Court

The law Bush signed that day is extraordinary: it is the only federal law *ever* enacted that criminally bans abortion procedures. And it is a law passed and signed in brazen defiance of the Supreme Court. For it was well known to policy makers that this abortion ban has the exact same constitutional deficiencies as the Nebraska law that the Supreme Court had struck down just three years before in *Stenberg v. Carhart:* it has no exception to save a woman's health, and only an inadequate exception to save her life, and the language of the law is so broad that it could ban techniques that doctors use regularly and safely even early in the second trimester. Besides placing the lives and health of women at risk, it puts doctors at risk of prosecution for providing safe, medically necessary care. In the Nebraska case, the court held that these restrictions are an "undue burden" on women. They are plainly bad policy, even if the law allowed them: who wants politicians telling our physicians what procedure to use on us for *any* surgery?

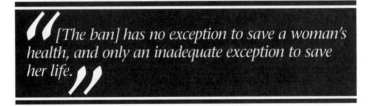

[The ban] has no exception to save a woman's health, and only an inadequate exception to save her life.

U.S. Attorney General John Ashcroft, for one. Immediately after the bill was signed, Ashcroft moved to assign enforcement of the law, which he said he intended to do vigorously. He directed the Justice Department's civil rights division to enforce the law, explaining that the law enlarges the civil rights of the fetus. . . .

Part of a Broader Campaign

The passage of the Partial-Birth Abortion Act was the culmination of a long-term strategy by right-wing extremists who have been working, ever since *Roe* to take away a woman's right to control her reproductive destiny. The abortion ban seemed at first to prohibit only a small number of rare, late-term procedures (just which procedures those *are* is a matter of debate, since, as Randall Terry, one of its supporters, says, "partial-birth abortion" is a public relations term, not a medical one). But in reality, the ban uses sweeping language that the Supreme Court has already recognized would affect a wide range of abortions.

The entire debate about so-called "partial-birth abortion" is part of a larger campaign to make *all* abortions illegal. It is a right-wing public relations strategy to manipulate language in order to sensationalize the abortion debate, to make the public believe that abortions are performed willy-nilly through all nine months of pregnancy by reckless physicians in cahoots with mothers who are intent on murdering their viable babies, and thereby bring both the public and formerly pro-choice politicians over to the anti-abortion camp. The incendiary language was designed to deceive the American people, and it worked. Dr. Leroy Carhart, the plaintiff in the case that struck down the previous ban, calls it "partial-truth abortion."

The War on Choice

And it is but one skirmish in a much larger war—the war on choice. The right to choose is not just about abortion, not by a long shot. It comprises the right to have full access to family planning information, health care, and products; the right to have children or not; sex education for young people that goes beyond the abstinence-only education being promoted by the right wing; and the right to medically accurate information about sexuality for the general public, too. Having the right to choose determines whether women will find an equal place at life's table, whether children will be truly valued, and whether everyone's personal liberties, privacy, and bodily integrity will be safeguarded against the ideology of the right.

Today's courts will almost certainly overrule the ban that President Bush signed into law. But the federal appeals courts are increasingly being filled with anti-choice ideologues, so who knows what will happen in the future? What those opposed to a woman's right to choose *hope* for is that by the time this law reaches the Supreme Court, there will be a different court, a court that, like the executive and legislative branches of the government, will be marching in lockstep with the anti-choice right. . . .

The anti-choice minority in this country is taking full advantage of the pro-choice majority's complacent assumption that with *Roe v. Wade* we won reproductive choice once and for all. Nothing could be further from the truth. In fact, *Roe v. Wade* so galvanized the anti-choice groups that almost as soon as the decision was handed down they began attacking reproductive rights on all fronts—in legislation, in the media, in the courts, in the state houses, in your hometown. This isn't an abortion war, it's a culture war, and its objective is to take away the economic, social, and political gains women have made since those years. Well funded and well organized, they are vocal, disciplined, and relentless in their assaults. They are creating a fearful atmosphere of sexual puritanism that hearkens back to the 1950s, and their goal is to return women to the position of powerlessness they occupied in that era.

A Backlash Against Women's Equality

To put it into its proper cultural and historical context, we must understand that the abortion ban—along with the many other attacks on women's reproductive rights—is part of a growing backlash against women's equality and freedom. Over the past fifty years, women have gained an astonishing amount of power, and *Roe v. Wade*, which gave women control over their fertility, was another major step toward empowerment. Not only did it legalize abortion but it became a symbol of our independence, because reproductive freedom is fundamental to a woman's aspirations—to education, financial stability, and self-determination. Reproductive freedom encompasses the right to freely and responsibly determine the number and spacing of our children. The simple ability to separate sex from childbearing gives women the power to control all other aspects of their lives. This is a profound shift in the gender power balance—a shift that most of us understand to be an advance in social justice, especially when we are thinking about ourselves and our own daughters. But it poses a threat to the status of the entrenched hierarchy.

That's why the right-wing extremists are so focused on taking away reproductive rights. And that's why they are using every weapon in their arsenals to ensure that politicians, judges, government appointees, and public health care agencies follow the anti-choice agenda. They are determined to take away not only the right to abortion but all reproductive rights.

12

Genetic Abnormality Does Not Always Justify Abortion

Shelley Burtt

Shelley Burtt has taught at Yale University and the London School of Economics and Political Science. She is the author of Virtue Transformed.

Genetic testing is often performed in order to prescreen abnormal fetuses for abortion. This practice appears to give parents control over their reproductive choices, but at what cost? Every human life has intrinsic value regardless of quality or genetic makeup. By judging disabled or "defective" persons as having lives not worth living, the opportunity to expand the scope of human freedom is denied and humanity is diminished.

What sort of life is worth living? Advances in medical technology have given Socrates' question a new, more poignant meaning. For the first time in history, we have the means to will the disappearance of those born disabled at the same time that we have the resources to enable these children to live better and longer lives than was ever possible before. How will we respond to these new cross-cutting possibilities? Genetic testing gives us the tools to choose in advance against certain sorts of lives. How are these tools to be used? What sort of lives are worth living?

As a bereaved parent of a child with Down syndrome, I am painfully aware that the life my son led for two and a half joyous years is a life that many individuals would cut short before it began. Although genetic testing is often presented as a service designed to reassure parents that their children-to-be are without congenital abnormalities, the practice in fact functions to prescreen "defective" fetuses for abortion. The assumption of most health care providers in the United States is that the successful diagnosis of a genetic anomaly provides an opportunity to "cure" a pathological condition. Once the arrival of a normally healthy baby is in doubt, the decision to abort is seen as rational and the opportunity to do so as fortunate.

For an anxious parent, genetic testing accompanied by the possibility of therapeutic abortion appears to enhance individual freedom by providing an additional measure of control over one's reproductive choices. But this perspective represents a woefully limited understanding of what it might mean to live as or with a person whose genetic makeup differs markedly from the general population and in a way that will to some extent impair his functioning. I'd like instead to explore what reasons we might have to resist the conclusion that a diagnosis of genetic abnormality is in itself a good reason to terminate a pregnancy and what cultural resources might be required to encourage this resistance.

> *Genetic testing gives us the tools to choose in advance against certain sorts of lives.*

My husband and I first welcomed Declan into our lives on a hot summer morning in July 1993. We had just come from the midwives' office where I had refused the genetic test (AFP) that screens for neural tube defects and would almost certainly have alerted us to our son's chromosomal abnormalities. Sitting on a bench outside Central Park, we asked ourselves, "What if there were a disability?" What use would we make of the information the test promised to provide? Although we come from different religious traditions (my husband is Jewish; I am Christian), we shared the view that the decision to create another human being was not conditional on the sort of human being that child turned out to be. For both of us, the child I was carrying was best understood as a gift we were being asked to care for, not a good we had the responsibility or right to examine for defects before accepting. With a blissfully innocent optimism, or perhaps an eerie prescience, we affirmed that day that we would love this child for who he was, whatever that turned out to be.

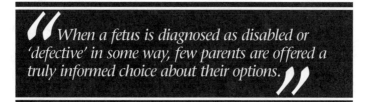

When a fetus is diagnosed as disabled or 'defective' in some way, few parents are offered a truly informed choice about their options.

Not every couple will willingly go through a pregnancy in ignorance of their fetus's health or future prospects, especially when the tests for a variety of disabling conditions are so readily available. What we can insist on, however, is a clear-eyed recognition of how genetic testing actually functions in our society and a greater commitment on the part of medical practitioners and prospective parents to fully reflect on the knowledge it provides. Whether or not to carry on with a pregnancy at all, let alone one which will result in the birth of a child with either moderate or profound disabilities, ought to be a decision made carefully and thoughtfully by the prospective parents of that child, not by strangers, legislators, or disability rights activists. But what does a good decision in these circumstances look like?

Understand All the Options

For many bioethicists, the watchword when it comes to difficult decision-making is individual autonomy. The role of the medical practitioner is not to prescribe a course of action but to provide the necessary information for the patient to decide what he or she truly wants to do. Yet, when a fetus is diagnosed as disabled or "defective" in some way, few parents are offered a truly informed choice about their options, as medical providers are rarely neutral when it comes to choosing between bringing an abnormal fetus to term or ending the pregnancy and "trying again." Because genetic abnormality is defined not as one characteristic with which a human being might be challenged but as a treatable medical problem, few parents faced with a positive diagnosis are invited to think beyond the now troubled pregnancy to the joys and rewards as well as the heartache and challenge that accepting and raising a child with special needs can bring.

More than this: to offer a therapeutic abortion as a "cure" for the diagnosed disability is deeply disingenuous. We do not cure cystic fibrosis or Down syndrome by ensuring that fetuses carrying this trait do not come to term; we simply destroy the affected entity. The service health care providers offer in this regard is more truthfully characterized as a form of eugenics, either medical (if driven by physicians' preferences) or personal (if driven by parents'). Physicians genuinely committed to patient autonomy in the context of genetic testing would not prejudge the worth or desirability of bearing a child whose genetic makeup was in some way abnormal. Instead, they would seek to ensure that parents truly understood what it meant to care for a child with special needs. This would mean, at a minimum, encouraging parents to inform themselves about the diagnosed condition, giving them the opportunity to speak to pediatricians familiar with the problem, and enabling them to meet with families already caring for children with this condition.

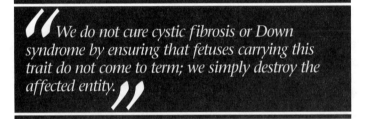

We do not cure cystic fibrosis or Down syndrome by ensuring that fetuses carrying this trait do not come to term; we simply destroy the affected entity.

Those who believe that the practice of genetic testing followed by selective abortion is an acceptable way of ensuring the birth of a healthy child often argue that the desire to parent a certain sort of child is not morally blameworthy. We can wish to be parents without wishing to be parents of a child with Fragile X syndrome or Tay-Sachs disease. Yet few who make this argument are willing to probe how our reproductive desires are constructed or at what point our desires become sufficiently self-reflective to be valid guides to action. On what basis do parents feel themselves "not ready" to parent a child with unexpectedly special needs? The picture they hold of a child's disabling trait and the effect it will have on the child and the family's life as a whole may be grounded in a volatile combination of fear and ignorance, not in some acquaintance with the actual life experiences of individuals already engaged in this task or deep reflection on the nature and purpose of parenting. It also seems likely that we cannot accurately assess in advance what challenges we are ready for. It is difficult to predict how we might grow and change in the face of seemingly adverse circumstances.

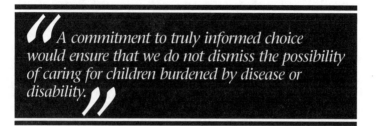

A commitment to truly informed choice would ensure that we do not dismiss the possibility of caring for children burdened by disease or disability.

Certain parents might feel they cannot responsibly continue a pregnancy in which an abnormality has been diagnosed because they lack the financial or emotional resources to care for such a child. But this assessment is not made in a vacuum. What we feel we can manage depends in part on the level of social and political support families with disabled children can expect to receive, support which in turn depends on the degree to which such lives are valued or appreciated by our community.

Social Attitudes Toward Disabilities Need to Change

The weight it is appropriate to give to parental desires in a reproductive context can perhaps be clarified by considering the internationally prevalent practice of sex-selective abortions. Parents around the world currently use the information derived from prenatal sonograms to advance their desire for a son by aborting female fetuses, a practice about which many physicians and most ethicists have grave moral reservations. Here, where parental desires are already considered suspect, the cultural construction of these desires and the appropriateness of resisting their expression is readily acknowledged. It is held to be an important part of making the world more just to change those cultural scripts which lead parents to prefer a son over a daughter so strongly that they will end a pregnancy rather than have a girl. We need to think critically and courageously about why a similar revaluation of social attitudes towards congenital disabilities is not also considered necessary.

I believe it is possible for some parents, after profound and prayerful reflection, to make the difficult decision that, all things considered, it is best for a child that it never be born. Incapacitating physical or mental deformity or the certainty of a life destroyed by a wasting disease are conditions which might conceivably, but not necessarily, call forth such a conclusion. But a judgement of this sort cannot be made with any fairness when speaking of disabilities such as spina bifida or Down syndrome where the quality of life available to the afflicted person is relatively high. A commitment to truly informed choice would ensure that we do not dismiss the possibility of caring for children burdened by disease or disability without an effort to appreciate and understand their possible lives.

But we need more than a commitment to truly informed choice if we are to create a world in which the birth of a disabled child is not thought of primarily as a stroke of bad luck, readily avoidable by more aggressive prenatal testing.

The lives of those whose capacities fall outside the normal range must be personally and socially recognized as independently valuable, not only worth living in themselves but worth living with.

As the parent of a disabled child, I have experienced first hand the transformed perspective on life possible when one is given the opportunity to live with those who confound our routine expectations, who have too much or too little of a range of expected human traits, who experience life in a way that must remain opaque to the majority of normally functional human beings. What my parents' generation would have called Declan's "mental retardation," we termed his "developmental disabilities." But what was neither retarded nor disabled was an infectious enthusiasm for life which illuminated any interaction with him, an ability to give and receive love that was uncomplicated by the egoism, self-awareness, or self-consciousness of a "typical" child. Parenting this child forced us to reconsider our conception of what qualities and capacities made life worth living; the joy my son clearly took in life and the joy he gave us compelled such a re-evaluation.

Human Life Has Intrinsic Value

But it is not enough to catalog the ways in which life with "them" is valuable for what it brings "us." The respect due to all persons by virtue of their humanity is not dependent on possessing only that sort of genetic makeup which guarantees normal human functioning. Our religious and political traditions teach that each human life has independent and intrinsic value. What would the consequences be of taking this truth seriously when we contemplated becoming parents?

> *The respect due to all persons by virtue of their humanity is not dependent on possessing only that sort of genetic makeup which guarantees normal human functioning.*

Such a commitment would have to call forth a profound re-assessment of the place of human will in the creation of human life. Both the cause of human freedom and of human equality have been admirably served by the ability, achieved only in this century, to choose to become parents. But we in the industrialized world now teeter on the brink of being able to choose what sort of children we want to become parents of. To some this capacity to control our destiny as parents is an almost unadulterated positive. One of the advantages of scientific progress is supposed to be the ability it gives humans to control their lives. Some make the point that being a good parent is hard enough without the additional burdens of severe or moderate disabilities to cope with. Others argue that it is cruel to bring a child into the world who will always be different, for whom the normal trials of life will be magnified hundreds of times. Why not, then, embrace the opportunity offered by advances in prenatal testing to discard those reproductive efforts we will experience as "disappointing," less than perfect, abnormal, or unhealthy? The most important reason is that sorting the results of the human reproductive process in this way ranks human beings according to their capacity to please their creators, fulfill their parents' dreams, or contribute to social productivity. This willingness to sit in judgement over the sorts of persons deserving a place in our moral communities closes down rather than enlarges the scope of human freedom. The ability to control one's destiny that science supposedly promotes turns out to be conditional on being the right sort of person.

As my younger sisters became pregnant in the wake of Declan's death, I hoped right along with them for a niece or nephew free from illness, defect, or developmental challenges.

The question is not whether it is right to desire a "normal" child, but how one ought to respond when genetic testing reveals that desire has been thwarted. To take steps at that point to abort the fetus and "try again" is not just to decide against being pregnant or in favor of "controlling one's life," it is to decide in advance and for another that a certain sort of life (a female one, a physically handicapped one, a mentally retarded one) is not worth living. The moral scope and impact of this decision appears to me far more troubling than a decision for or against parenthood based solely on a positive pregnancy test. Postponing an abortion decision until one knows what sort of child has been created places relative weights on human beings: some are more worthy of living, of being cared for, of being cherished, than others.

Having cared, however briefly, for a special needs child, I do not belittle the level of care and commitment called forth by the opportunity to parent a child or adult with moderate to severe disabilities. But I remain deeply skeptical that the best response to these challenges is the one currently favored by the Western medical establishment: to treat congenital imperfections as we do infectious diseases and to seek their cure by their eradication. Rather we need, through a genuine encounter with those whose identities are shaped but never fully encompassed by their bodies' imperfections, to rethink our willingness not only to live with the disabled but to live with unchosen obligations. Our cultural assumptions to the contrary, living a good and rich life does not require and is not identical with complete control of its circumstances. In fact, the aspiration for such "freedom" dishonors a fundamental aspect of the human condition. To those willing to recognize the essential humanity of every possible child, sometimes to choose not to know—not to act on what we do know—will be the best choice of all.

13

Genetic Screening for Abnormality Is Morally Justified

John Gillott

John Gillott is the policy officer at the Genetic Interest Group in London, which is a British national alliance of organizations that promotes awareness of and quality services for people affected by genetic disorders.

A fear exists that modern genetic screening for fetal abnormalities is a form of eugenics that was used in the past to rid the population of certain groups of people. However, the new genetics focuses on medical diseases rather than on race or social differences. Parents' decisions to terminate a pregnancy following genetic testing are framed by their own conditions and abilities, not on moral judgment about people living with disabilities.

The decision to undergo genetic testing during pregnancy rests with the woman, usually after consultation with her partner. When there is a family history of a genetic condition, the initiative, the initial suggestion that testing could be used, will usually come from the woman. In the case of population screening it is health professionals who take the initiative. For example couples might be offered screening with the aim of determining whether they are carriers for a condition; if they are and a pregnancy is established, antenatal testing will be offered. . . .

However the issue is posed, the primary choice, in screening and also in patient-initiated testing, is to avoid the birth of

John Gillott, "Screening for Disability: A Eugenic Pursuit," *Journal of Medical Ethics*, October 2001. Copyright © 2001 by the British Medical Association. Reproduced by permission.

a child with a genetic condition. Is this eugenic? There are a number of variations of the argument which suggest that it is. These different aspects of argument are put with varying degrees of vigour by different critics of antenatal screening and selective termination, and clearly, whether or not these procedures are thought to be "eugenic" will depend on what that emotive term is taken to mean.

What Is Eugenics?

In this brief presentation of the arguments I cannot hope to do justice to the full range of opinion and writings on the subject. I do hope, however, to establish that the values of modern medical genetics are fundamentally different from those of the main strands in historical eugenics, and that approval for genetic testing prior to birth is compatible with equal treatment for people living with disabilities.

[The English anthropologist] Francis Galton defined eugenics as the scientific study of the biological and social factors which improve or impair the inborn qualities of human beings and of future generations. Such study suggests a practice of eugenics. A modern definition might be any policy that alters the composition of the human gene pool. The philosopher Philip Kitcher develops this interpretation in his thoughtful book *The Lives to Come: The Genetic Revolution and Human Possibilities*. He then subdivides the notion into different types. Interestingly, he also characterises doing nothing when we have the ability to do something as eugenic. At this point the critics of genetic testing part company with him. For them, eugenics is about humanity changing the gene pool, specifically reducing the incidence of genetic disorders, whether it is government policy or the aggregate of individual decisions that brings this about.

The Fear of Eugenics Programs

Both Kitcher's and the critics' notions have their merits. But posing the issue in such a general way also tends to obscure crucial differences between historical eugenics and modern genetics. At the turn of the century there was a widespread belief that genetics influenced morals and personality traits. The preoccupation was with controlling the spread of these traits, rather than medical conditions. The dominant strand in eugenics of old was a state-led drive to alter the gene pool, in some cases by coercive measures. It was used to justify the sterilisation, and even murder, of people classed as mentally insane and genetically inferior.

At the time, not enough was known about genetics and disease/behaviour to highlight the scientifically irrational character of many of the eugenic proposals. Enough was known, however, about population genetics by 1920 to invalidate, on scientific, never mind humane grounds, eugenic arguments for sterilisation. That such programmes continued regardless highlights perhaps the most important point to understand about the dominant strand of old eugenics: it was driven neither by science nor by humanitarian concern but by a strong political belief and fear—of national, racial, and social decline. As the historian Daniel Kevles puts it, using the example of Britain at the turn of the century: "To many British, the general fibre of the nation—its overall moral character, intelligence, energy, ambition, and capacity to compete in the world—was declining".

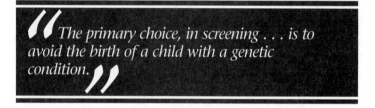

The primary choice, in screening . . . is to avoid the birth of a child with a genetic condition.

After the second world war, eugenic practices continued for some time, up until the 1970s in the case of Sweden. Eugenicists sought to pursue their goals through the new field of reproductive and genetic counselling, and some still believe that the moral worth and future of nations depend upon genetics. But in my view the predominant ethos of all work in human genetics today, and in medical genetics in particular, has little or nothing in common with historical eugenics.

The new genetics is concerned more with identifiable medical diseases than with personality traits and behaviours. It represents a biological approach to biological problems, not a reductionist approach to the whole human being. This is not to say that modern behaviour genetics and the genetics of mental health are marginal fields of inquiry; they are not. But leading researchers in the field understand the limited contribution of many different genes. Their study is primarily individual variation, not purported race or social-group differences, and very few working in the field link genetics to ideas of racial or national success and failure. Finally, these areas of genetics do not impinge on services offered prior to implantation or birth, and are unlikely to do so for the foreseeble future.

Genetic Screening Does Not Devalue People with Disabilities

Some within the disability rights movement might accept the distinction I have drawn, but continue to object to antenatal testing and screening because they believe it necessarily devalues those living with the condition. Focusing on the motivations of parents in the first instance, I believe that this is wrong, and that the critics are guilty of conflating impairment and the moral status of people—something they often accuse supporters of testing and screening programmes of doing.

I have located modern genetics within the traditions of humanistic medicine. Clearly, selective termination, a possible outcome of one aspect of genetic science, is not a "cure" or treatment. I would argue, however, that parental attitudes towards fetal abnormality are framed by attitudes towards illness and not unreasonable expectations about the impact of such genetic disorders on their own and their children's lives. If they choose to terminate an affected pregnancy they are making a judgment about impairment, which is the level at which antenatal selection operates, and a guess about the life they, and a child with the particular condition, would have, given existing levels of medical knowledge and social support. That judgment is a relative one, i.e., that life without the condition is better than life with it. Parents are not, as the caricature sometimes has it, saying that life with a genetic disorder is not worth living or is too terrible to contemplate. And certainly, they do not see themselves as making a moral judgment about the worth or rights of people living with that genetic condition.

14

Human Embryo Experimentation Can Be Morally Justified

Michael J. Meyer and Lawrence J. Nelson

Michael J. Meyer is an associate professor and department chair of philosophy at Santa Clara University in California. Lawrence J. Nelson is a lecturer of philosophy at Santa Clara University and has served as a bioethics consultant to the National Institutes of Health.

Human embryos have a weak, though genuine, moral status because they are alive and valued, but they are not moral agents (human beings capable of sentience). In other words, the embryo is not a person, but because many people value it, it should be treated with respect. Destroying embryos in the pursuit of legitimate research can be seen as morally justified, therefore. In fact, people often destroy what they respect. For example, Native Americans respected the animals they depended upon for food; to show their reverence, the Indians conducted hunting rituals that gave thanks to the animals for giving up their lives so that people could live. So long as the two people who created the embryo willingly agree to donate the embryo to science, human embryo experimentation can be said to be justified.

How can one have moral respect for something that one intentionally destroys? This perplexing question is pointedly raised by several commentators on the ethics of human stem cell and embryo research when they claim that extracorporeal

Michael J. Meyer and Lawrence J. Nelson, "Respecting What We Destroy: Reflections on Human Embryo Research," *Hastings Center Report*, January/February 2001. Copyright © 2001 by The Hastings Center. Reproduced by permission.

embryos at one and the same time merit "profound respect," "respect . . . for [their] special character," or "special respect," and yet remain suitable for use in scientific research that results in their destruction. Daniel Callahan [senior fellow at the Harvard Medical School], among others, has puzzled about how the extracorporeal embryo can be both "entitled to profound respect" and also sacrificed "in deference to the requirements of research." The puzzle for Callahan, and for us here, is how we can, without a tragic disingenuousness, accede to "the killing of something for which [we] claim to have a profound respect." The puzzle raises two questions: Does not having an attitude of respect for something rule out its ultimate destruction? Second, even if this is not so, is not the research use and destruction of embryos "more honestly done by simply stripping [these] embryos of any value at all?"

Our answer to both questions is no. What respect requires can be an alternative both to a prohibition on destruction and to a moral license to kill. We will argue that a genuine moral respect for embryos can be joined—without incongruity but not without careful attention to how that respect is displayed—with their use and destruction in legitimate research. This is of course not meant to be a description of the moral attitudes that people typically have about embryos. Our conclusion is rather an evocation of a moral ideal especially worthy of recognition at a time when research using human embryos is likely to escalate.

Before taking up the moral compatibility between respecting something and destroying it, we first provide a brief account of moral status in general and then address the particular moral status of embryos. The moral status of an entity must be clarified before the moral permissibility of its intentional destruction can be ascertained. It is to the question of moral status, then, that we turn first.

Moral Status

There are nonmoral uses of the idea of respect—like the respect one might have for a heavyweight champion's left hook or a scholar's opinion. An agent evinces *moral* respect, however, when he or she sincerely considers and actually treats an entity as worthy of some degree of deference, reverence, or regard. Plainly, this kind of respect is dependent on a reckoning of the entity's moral status. An entity toward which moral agents have direct obligations, or whose needs, interests, or well-being require protection, for example, will also command respect. Moral agents clearly have a rather high moral status, and they correspondingly deserve very significant moral respect.

However, moral respect should not be collapsed into an account of respect for moral agents or their characteristics. Humans who are not agents or not yet agents, sentient creatures, other living things, species, and biotic communities are all sometimes said to have moral status and deserve moral respect. Of course, if such widely varying kinds of entities are accorded moral status, the notions of moral status and respect must admit of degrees. Plainly, too, people differ in what they assign status and accord respect to. Nonetheless, any attribution of moral status, however weak, must be taken seriously by others.

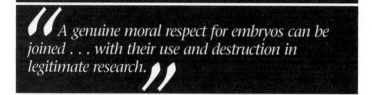

A genuine moral respect for embryos can be joined . . . with their use and destruction in legitimate research.

We employ the method of ascertaining moral status recently elaborated by [philosophy professor] Mary Anne Warren, who has argued convincingly that no one criterion can determine moral status. In fact, for Warren, a judgment about an entity's moral status involves seven different principles, which include both intrinsic and relational properties of the entity in question. In abbreviated form, Warren's seven principles are: (1) *respect for life:* living organisms may not be killed or harmed without good reasons; (2) *anti-cruelty:* sentient beings ought not to be killed or subjected to pain unless there is no other way of furthering goals that are both consistent with the other principles and important to entities that have higher moral status than can be based on sentience alone; (3) *agent's rights:* moral agents have full and equal moral rights, including rights to life and liberty; (4) *human rights:* within the limits of their capacities, human beings capable of sentience but not moral agency have the same moral rights as moral agents; (5) *ecological importance:* ecologically important entities (living and nonliving) may have a stronger moral status than they would independent of their relationship to the ecosystem; (6) *interspecific communities:* animals that are part of a human community may have stronger moral status than they would standing alone; (7) *tran-

sitivity of respect: within the limits of the above principles and to the extent that is reasonable, moral agents should respect one another's attributions of moral status.

Respect

Our account of moral respect will draw on Warren's work. In this account, moral agents have the highest moral status and possess full and equal basic moral rights. An individual who displays only minimal consciousness has the same basic moral rights and status as an agent, even though he lacks those rights his diminished capacities render irrelevant. Nonhuman but sentient creatures possess a moral status that is significant but typically less than that of humans. Other, nonsentient living entities have even lower status but still merit some, even if in most cases quite minimal, moral respect.

If Warren's account is right, human embryos have a weak moral status and deserve a weak but genuine moral respect. The moral status of embryos does not, contrary to the suggestion of some, rest exclusively on their being the result of reproductive activity. Rather, the human embryo has a claim to some moral status both in virtue of being alive and in virtue of Warren's rule of the "transitivity of respect." Although frozen embryos are in a state of suspended animation, they are still living entities, and purely gratuitous harm to or destruction of a living thing is, many would say, clearly morally problematic. When a living thing is harmed or destroyed there must be some reasonable justification for doing so. Thus while the claim that life itself is worthy of moral respect is surely controversial, it is hardly unusual, and indeed seems rather plausible if moral respect is held to admit of different levels.

The moral status of embryos also turns on the fact that, in addition to being alive, they are valued, in some cases very highly, by many people. The value ascribed to an embryo covers a wide range, of course; it is sometimes essentially given the full worth and status of a moral agent, sometimes a very high status but not at every stage the equal of a moral agent, and sometimes only very modest moral status. Some hold that an extracorporeal human embryo naturally engenders a sense of wonder, or that it is a thing of beauty. What gives rise to these reactions provides a reason to hold that the extracorporeal embryo has some modest moral status. One might, for instance, have a sense of wonder about embryos because of the simple realization that an embryo is, in some rough sense, "the stuff of life." Its beauty alone is also a distinct reason to accord it some moral status.

The transitivity principle does not depend on a defense of any particular view an agent might hold about the embryo's moral status. The whole point of the transitivity principle is that the actual valuations of other agents merit respect even when one does not share their valuations. According some respect to the value judgments of others does not entail that one shares those value judgments, even less that one has abandoned one's own values, but simply that one has some respect for the individuals who *do* have those values. Stones may be uninteresting to us, but we nonetheless should recognize some obligation to protect rock formations that are sacred to others, as Uluru is for Australian aboriginals or Shiprock for the Navajo. Respect for the moral agency of others requires us to not dismiss their views lightly. Demonstrating this respect is one aspect of showing respect for one's fellow agents. To suggest instead that moral views that depart from one's own should be dismissed is not only to court dogmatism, but also to fail to establish reasonable and principled common ground with those who have divergent views of complex moral problems.

> *Human embryos have a weak moral status and deserve a weak but genuine moral respect.*

Surely, then, there is good reason to say that the extracorporeal embryo has some moral status and is worthy of some moral respect. More specifically, our interpretation of Warren's account leads us to conclude that its status is weak or modest. The only intrinsic property that provides a reason to grant it moral status is its being alive. The embryo is neither an agent, a human being capable of sentience but not agency, a nonhuman sentient creature, nor an entity of ecological significance. Nor is an embryo a person, or an early stage of a person, in the typical understandings, both metaphysical and moral, of the muddled term "person." One oft-noted reason it isn't is that an embryo prior to the formation of the "primitive streak" (which usually appears around fourteen days of development) is not clearly even an *individual*, as it can still be divided into twins. Personhood is usually taken to imply individuality. Another reason is that, if an embryo is maintained outside a woman's body and those who provided the gametes for it have not decided to permit its development in a womb, it is not effectively a stage in the early development of a person. Put differently, an extracorporeal embryo—whether used in research, discarded, or kept frozen—is simply not a precursor to any ongoing personal narrative. An embryo properly starts on that trajectory only when the gamete sources intentionally have it placed in a womb.

We recognize that reasonable people will continue to disagree about the moral status of embryos. Indeed, the very recent appearance of the extracorporeal embryo (it did not exist before the 1970s) provides reason to think that disagreement about its moral status is more than understandable. Our goal, however, is not to provide a knock-down argument about the moral status of the embryo, but to show how one systematic, reasonable view on moral status in general can be used to defend the moral propriety of destroying embryos that truly deserve respect. For this defense to succeed, it is necessary that the status of the embryo be assessed as only modest or weak.

"Special" Respect

Nevertheless, possession of even weak *moral* status supports the claim that embryos deserve "special" respect. Something's entitlement to even weak moral status requires that there be sincere moral deliberation about its treatment. Those who doubt the force of this point underestimate the importance of the line between the moral and nonmoral. The very presence of moral status demands sincere and genuine reflection on questions like: What level of respectful treatment do I owe this entity? What would a morally admirable person do to this entity, and what should I in good conscience refuse to do to it? In contrast, all such questions are simply beside the point for entities without moral status.

When we are considering an entity that has any moral status, destruction, harm, or any other disrespectful treatment cannot be justified by our self-interest alone. Our account of the moral status of human embryos entails that they deserve some respect in all contexts, even when they are destroyed for good reason. Whenever the forces of moral deliberation are called into play on behalf of an entity having even weak moral status, reasonable and conscientious persons clearly are required to give due regard to the entity in question as well as to the manner in which their actions regarding it affect their own moral character.

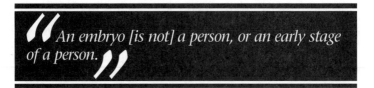

An embryo [is not] a person, or an early stage of a person.

The moral respect an agent has for something or someone is demonstrated in two fundamental ways: in what the agent does or refuses to do with the object of respect, and in the attitudes the agent adopts in relation to that which he or she respects. Behavior must be consistent with attitude; someone cannot legitimately claim he or she holds a respectful attitude about something while his or her behavior clearly manifests indifference, disregard, or contempt. Morally respectful behavior can assume a variety of forms: addressing the respected entity in a certain manner, protecting and preserving it from destruction or degradation, thinking of it or talking about it in terms that accurately reflect its value, and encouraging or requiring others to behave respectfully. The precise forms of respectful behavior adopted by an agent should also be congruent with the degree of respect owed to the particular object in question. To solve the puzzle of how we can show respect for what we destroy, we must recognize the moral weight of both the sincerely respectful attitude of the destroying agent toward the destroyed object, as well as the purposefully adopted behavioral manifestations of this attitude.

Sometimes people destroy something *because* they respect it, as when a sacred artifact is destroyed to prevent its being treated in a profane way. In contrast, embryos are destroyed in the course of research *in spite of* the respect they deserve. Destroying an object in spite of the respect it is owed raises the tension we seek to resolve. To illustrate how the tension might be resolved, we offer some actual examples of people who have destroyed what they truly respect.

Destroying What Is Respected

A variety of Native American hunting cultures manifested a "very close relationship between man and game animals" that was grounded in their religious beliefs as well as in the ritual attitudes they maintained and practices they observed with respect to these animals. For these peoples, all living beings are "associated with and related to one another socially and sociably," as humans are to each other. They did not see animals as objects, but as "fellows with whom the individual or band may have a more or less advantageous relationship." These Native Americans also believed supernatural masters or owners of the game animals existed who cared about the way the animals were treated and would punish hunters who kill excessively or show other disrespectful behavior toward the animals.

The Cree and Micmac cultures, to pick two examples, expressed their respect for the animals they destroyed in a wide variety of ways. Some addressed the animal by a familial name such as "Grandmother" or "Cousin" or by an honorary title like "Chief's Son" or "Four-Legged Human." They demonstrated respect or esteem by killing animals only with aboriginal weapons and by making a conciliatory speech to the animal, either before or after killing it (and sometimes both), "by which the hunter sincerely apologizes for the necessity of his act." They maintained a reverent atmosphere while eating a bear and carefully avoided wasting any of it—even avoiding spilling into the fire any soup made from the animal. Finally, they showed respect for the animal's remains by never throwing its bones into the fire or giving them to the dogs, and sometimes they went so far as to bury the animal's bones in anatomical order.

The Japanese practice of *mizuko kuyo* can be understood as another demonstration of respect for what is destroyed, in this case the aborted human fetus. *Mizuko kuyo* includes a variety of spiritual rituals initiated primarily by women as memorial services for their aborted fetuses. These rituals include saying prayers, making floral offerings, burning incense, lighting candies, creating wooden plaques called *ema* that carry prayers for, and messages to, the fetuses (such as "please sleep peacefully" or "please forgive me"), and making reverential bows to the *mizuko jizo*, a statuary image that represents the soul of the deceased fetus and the deity that cares for departed children. One commentator has noted that although the content of the ritual varies widely, they all aim "uniformly to comfort and honor" the spirits of the aborted fetuses. In addition, some of those who perform *mizuko kuyo* rituals do so partly because they wish to make a public demonstration that they acted responsibly. Others have the "desire to register publicly their belief that they did not abort unfeelingly or callously." Older women especially do not perform the ritual "in shame or fear" so much as to "give public recognition to an act that for them was both sorrowful and unavoidable."

Naomi Wolf has argued that the struggle for abortion rights should be placed within a moral framework that urges all discussions about "destroy[ing] a manifestation of life" be characterized by "grief and respect." For those who believe that "abortion is killing and yet [are] still prochoice," Wolf suggests that they engage in "acts of redemption, or what the Jewish mystical tradition calls *tikkun*, or 'mending.'" She provides several examples of such acts, one of which is to suggest that mothers or fathers who were involved in an abortion can "remember the aborted child every time [they are] tempted to be less than loving—and give renewed love to [a] living child." Such acts of *tikkun*, as well as the practice of *mizuko kuyo*, are manifestations of genuine respect for the aborted fetus, even if that respect was by itself not enough to lead a woman to forgo the abortion.

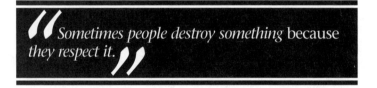

Sometimes people destroy something because they respect it.

The contemporary treatment of human cadavers in medical schools provides another example of treating with respect that which is destroyed. All known societies have had customs delineating the proper treatment of the bodies of the dead. These customs mostly are characterized by the value and respect paid to the bodies and the consequent revulsion experienced by encountering desecration of corpses or other acts of disrespect. Antigone defied at great risk her king's order to leave her brother's body unburied, and therefore in disgrace, in order to obey what she saw as her moral duty to bury him with respect. Dissection of human cadavers for educational or scientific purposes was widely condemned for hundreds of years, although the need for dissection led physicians and others to rob graves or to use bodies unclaimed by relatives. Dissection was so disfavored in the United States that one state legally banned it until 1887, and another made it a "punishment" for having been killed while dueling.

Respect for human cadavers is ethically grounded in the

very close identification of persons and their bodies and in the association of the human form with living human beings themselves. "While the body retains a recognizable form, even in death, it commands the respect of identity," notes William May. "No longer a human presence, it still reminds us of the presence that once was utterly inseparable from it." In addition, cadavers are especially honored by those who had personal relationships with the persons while alive, and others are bound by the transitivity principle to respect both the cadaver and those who hold it in special regard. The respect that is owed to cadavers is reflected in the honorific rituals of institutions which make scientific and educational use of cadavers:

> While [the memorial services held prior to burial or cremation of dissected remains] take a variety of forms, their aim is to honor those who have donated their bodies to an anatomy department for the purposes of teaching and research. This serves as a formal and public demonstration of anatomy departments' appreciation for such bequests. Whether secular or ecumenical, such services bring together the altruism of the donors, the gratitude of the students and faculty, and the memories of close relatives and friends.

In addition, students and researchers should, and do, show respect for cadavers during their use and destruction of them.

No Inherent Contradiction

The conscientious treatment shown to dissected cadavers clearly displays the respect that they are widely thought to be owed. Likewise the redemptive acts of *tikkun* and the rituals of *mizuko kuya* deserve to be understood in light of the recognition that the persons who engage in them are showing a special respect for what they have intentionally destroyed. And the Native American rituals have meaning only given the understanding that the hunter who has destroyed the animals did have some deep and genuine respect for them.

Now it is not our present point to defend either these specific practices or the complex set of moral evaluations out of which they arise. Instead, we want first to make the more limited point that there is no inherent conceptual contradiction or severe moral dilemma involved in the general idea of showing respect for what one destroys. The examples afford a few authentic instances of the general practice of respecting what one destroys.

Second, although we do not wish to argue for the precise form of respectful, compensatory acknowledgment for either animals, fetuses, cadavers, or even embryos, the examples provide a rough idea of some of the typical features of respecting what one destroys. They suggest that respecting what one destroys should include an attitude of regret, and some sense of loss, conjoined with a display of that respect. Respecting what is destroyed should include an attitude of regret and loss because the thing one has intentionally destroyed does in fact have moral value. Even the gains reaped through its destruction do not preclude honest and open acknowledgment of the regret and loss one should feel about it.

Gamete Sources Have a Choice

The persons most humanly and morally connected to any particular extracorporeal embryo are the individual women and men from whom the gametes came. These persons have a special connection to any embryo they create for two reasons. First, as the embryo is wholly constituted by the gametes that were part of, indeed a genetic representation of, the persons from whom they came, these gamete sources are uniquely connected to the embryo biologically and ontologically. Without these gametes the particular embryo in question simply would not exist.

Second, the gamete sources also have a genuine moral connection to their embryos. This may be grounded in either a particular interest they might take in those of their embryos not designated for reproductive uses, or a potentially profound interest they might take in an embryo that is designated for reproduction. Most persons care deeply if their gametes are used, by themselves or others, to create a child, and being a genetic parent can understandably be linked in deep ways to an individual's sense of identity and of the meaning of life. In a clearly different but still meaningful way, gamete sources might well care about how their embryo is used by others for research purposes. They might believe, for example, that the embryo has independent moral value. They might also feel that it simply belongs to him or her and that no one else should be using it. Furthermore, it is implausible that someone other than a gamete source would have a more significant moral connection to a particular embryo.

As a direct result of the special biological, ontological, and moral connection between embryos and the persons whose gametes are used to create them, the latter should jointly exercise the right of exclusive control over the disposition of those embryos, whether they be used immediately or later for personal reproductive use, donated to others for reproductive purposes, donated to research, or just discarded. This deep interest in the valuation of and control over an embryo is closely related to an individual's interest in and right to make intimate, personal decisions. This interest should prevail over conflicting views others may have of the embryo's moral value or of what may be done with it. Therefore, the voluntary, informed consent of the gamete sources is morally required for any disposition of their embryos, and others ought to respect the terms and conditions the gamete sources place on this disposition.

> // The contemporary treatment of human cadavers in medical schools provides [an] example of treating with respect that which is destroyed. //

The gamete sources may confer on their own embryos a moral status higher than the minimum status we argued for earlier in this paper. If they do, they might refuse either to donate their embryos for research or to destroy any of them and might try instead to bring all of them eventually to birth. Treating their embryos this way violates none of the moral duties they owe to others. Given their prerogative to grant their own embryos more than minimal moral status, the gamete sources are not morally obliged to permit their embryos to be used by someone else for reproduction or research. Put differently, no one should be morally or legally compelled either to become a genetic parent through use of his or her embryos or to donate one's own embryo for any legitimate or worthy use by another. If the case in favor of giving all embryos higher moral status and more respectful treatment could be made convincingly to others, then many more, maybe even most, gamete sources would refuse to donate embryos to research. Still, no moral wrong would thereby be done to researchers or to humankind, even though a potential good would be delayed or forgone.

While the gamete sources may stipulate special restrictions on how an embryo is to be treated, there are also some general, base-line requirements for the treatment of an embryo. No moral agent can properly deem an extracorporeal embryo— whether someone else's or hers—morally worthless. Although the *disposition* of extracorporeal embryos "belongs" to the gamete sources who created them, the embryos are not like simple proprietary objects that can be regarded by their owners as valueless. As we argued above embryos have genuine, if modest, moral status and deserve genuine respect both because they are alive and because they are regarded by others as morally valuable.

If embryos are acknowledged to have only a weak moral status, nothing wrong is done to any embryo if the gamete sources voluntarily donate them, with a respectful acknowledgment of their moral status, for use in legitimate research— research, that is, that utilizes sound scientific methodology and design and possesses the reasonable promise of generating significant knowledge, whether theoretical or practical in nature. While significance is surely a matter of degree, significant knowledge is at least not trivial. It would not, for instance, be clearly unnecessary repetition of established results. In addition, legitimate research neither involves morally objectionable acts nor is predominantly intended to generate publicity, economic value, or achieve some other end at the direct expense of developing generalizable knowledge.

> *Donating embryos for [legitimate] research, even though it involves their destruction, can be consistent with genuine respect for them.*

Donating embryos for such research, even though it involves their destruction, can be consistent with genuine respect for them, because of their weak moral status. Such use and destruction would be by itself disrespectful if it were moral agents who were used in research, but for embryos destruction is not inherently unacceptable, *provided* both that the gamete sources consent to this use and that the extracorporeal embryo receives respectful treatment, proportional to its moral status. A variety of attitudes and practices can demonstrate respectful acknowledgment of the moral status of extracorporeal embryos. In the context of research with embryos, both gamete sources and researchers are the parties most immediately obligated to make such respectful acknowledgment. The duties of the two might also be linked in the following way: examples of how researchers might show respect, or avoid showing disrespect, can be understood as cases of what gamete sources could request, or require, from the researchers to whom they donate their extracorporeal embryos.

Restrictions

Examples of restrictions on the treatment of embryos that would show respect for them (which are independent of justifications for their destruction) would include the following: (1) human extracorporeal embryos should be used in research only if the research goals cannot be obtained with other methods; (2) the use of extracorporeal embryos more than fourteen days old should be avoided or diminished, since this point is regarded by some as the morally significant onset of embryonic individuation; (3) researchers should avoid considering extracorporeal embryos as property and in particular should avoid buying and selling them; (4) researchers should recognize that the destruction of extracorporeal embryos provides a reason for them to have and demonstrate some sense of regret or loss. Further, handling extracorporeal embryos with respect in the lab should never be an empty or insincere gesture but might include both acquiring only the minimum number of embryos required to achieve the research goals and disposing of the remains of used embryos in a way respectful of their status (for example, the remains might be treated as if they were corpses and be buried or cremated).

Thus while the embryo's moral status need not prevent us from killing it, it should nevertheless have some practical deterrent effect against killing it, since it requires that the destruction be for justifiable reasons, and that the destruction and eventual disposal in some way reflect the seriousness of the event. In our view no one ought to kill extracorporeal embryos for trivial reasons or in ways that would in fact fail to show respect for them. There is, in general, no reason to suppose that *any* level of moral status and respect should have a practical deterrent effect against *every* form of killing—even moral agents may be killed in self-defense. In short, the level of moral status and respect due to any particular entity will establish the level of justification required to render killing that entity permissible.

We leave open for further specification precisely what displays of respect are appropriate for embryos, but there must be some such displays or the accompanying use of extracorporeal embryos will be unethical.

Unresolved Issues

Our attempt to show how we can reasonably combine genuine moral respect for extracorporeal embryos with their intentional destruction leaves a number of related issues deliberately untouched. These include: (1) the relationship between the moral status of the extracorporeal embryo and its legal status, and whether the law ought to enforce certain restrictions that would reflect respectful treatment (for example, banning commercial trade in embryos); (2) a set of further moral considerations, such as how the practices involved in respecting what one destroys help deepen habits of moral imagination and other subtleties of moral character; (3) whether some proponents of research distort its moral and practical value in order to justify the use of embryos; (4) what to do, morally or legally, if the gamete sources disagree on the disposition of their extracorporeal embryos; and (5) whether the intentional creation of embryos exclusively for research purposes can be morally justified.

We have sought to parry Callahan's suggestion that the use and destruction of human embryos is best justified "by simply stripping embryos of any value at all." Instead we have argued that given the minimal but real moral respect owed to an embryo, there can be, and ought to be, some display of respect whenever they are used, but that the destruction of an embryo need not display disrespect for it. Moreover, while the display of such respect could range widely in form and content, ignoring this display is in all likelihood a sign of a hardening of the heart that need not be part of our scientific progress.

15

Embryonic Stem Cell Research Is Unethical

Richard M. Doerflinger

Richard M. Doerflinger is the deputy director of the Secretariat for Pro-life Activities at the U.S. Conference of Catholic Bishops.

Embryonic stem cell research involves the destruction of human embryos. Harming a human being in the pursuit of medical knowledge is unethical, regardless of the resulting benefit to others. The embryo is the first stage of human life and as such deserves respect and recognition as a member of the human family. The argument that only embryos already slated for destruction would be used for research is itself immoral and implies that condemned prisoners or terminally ill patients could also be used for experimentation. Killing human embryos for research or any other purpose is intrinsically wrong.

The central ethical issue raised by [human embryonic stem cell] research is raised whenever proponents of unlimited research freedom complain that ethical restraints get in the way of "progress." This tension between technical advance and respect for research subjects is at least as old as modern medicine itself. As soon as Western thinkers began to see medicine as a science that could advance and acquire new knowledge, the temptation arose of using human beings as mere means to this end.

When Dr. Claude Bernard sounded an alarm against this temptation in the 19th century, the preferred victims were pris-

Richard M. Doerflinger, testimony before U.S. Senate Subcommittee on Science, Technology and Space, Committee on Commerce, Science and Transportation, Washington, DC, September 29, 2004.

oners convicted of serious crimes. He insisted that the physician must not deliberately do harm to any human being simply to acquire knowledge that may help others:

> The principle of medical and surgical morality, therefore, consists in never performing on man an experiment that might be harmful to him to any extent, even though the result might be highly advantageous to science, i.e., to the health of others. But performing experiments and operations exclusively from the point of view of the patient's own advantage does not prevent their turning out profitably to science.

In 1865, Dr. Bernard was already making the important distinction between therapeutic and nontherapeutic experimentation. The fact that an experiment may benefit the research subject is only one moral requirement among others; but it is one thing to provide a human being with an experimental treatment whose outcome may also help in treating others in the future, and quite another thing simply to use him or her as a means, imposing significant risk of harm on him or her solely to benefit others.

The Need for Ethical Safeguards in Human Research

In the Nuremberg Code, the United States and its allies responded to the horrors of the Nazi war crimes by restating this principle, to ensure that human dignity would not again be trampled on in the pursuit of medical knowledge. Among other things, the Code declared: "No experiment should be conducted where there is an a priori reason to believe that death or disabling injury will occur. . . ."

This Code inspired many later declarations, including the "Declaration of Helsinki" first approved by the World Medical Association in 1964. Here the key principle is:

> In medical research on human subjects, considerations related to the well-being of the human subject should take precedence over the interests of science and society.

The Helsinki declaration noted that this principle must apply to *all* human beings, and that "some research populations," including those who cannot give consent for themselves, "need special protection." It seems this principle was intended to encompass the unborn, as the same organization's statement on the ethics of the practicing physician, the "Declaration of Geneva," had the physician swear that "I will maintain the utmost respect for *human life, from the time of conception.*"

Despite these solemn declarations, American scientists and others dazzled by visions of technical progress have always been tempted to endorse a utilitarian approach to ethics, and to treat helpless or unpopular members of the human race as mere means to their ends.

> *In medical research on human subjects, considerations related to the well-being of the human subject should take precedence over the interests of science and society.*

In the Tuskegee syphilis experiment, for example, hundreds of poor black sharecroppers were deliberately left with untreated syphilis for over twenty years to observe the course of their disease. This was no isolated aberration but a sustained, decades-long study conducted with U.S. government support. A report filed by the Public Health Service at the end of the process, in 1953 (years *after* Nuremberg!), shows no trace of ethical concern—rather, the authors comment favorably on how subjects were encouraged to comply with the study by the offering of "incentives"—including the offer of free burial assistance once they died from their untreated syphilis! The authors concluded: "As public health workers accumulate experience and skill in this type of study, not only should the number of such studies increase, but a maximum of information will be gained from the efforts expended."

There were indeed more such studies. We need only think of the study at Willowbrook children's home, where retarded children in the 1960s were deliberately injected with hepatitis virus to study ways of preventing spread of the disease. One justification offered by the researchers was that hepatitis was so common in the institution that these children probably would have been exposed to it anyway—an argument we now see in the embryo research debate, when researchers insist that the human embryos they destroy probably would have been discarded anyway. Or we can look to our government's Cold War studies on the effects of radiation using unsuspecting military and civilian subjects, conducted from the 1940s to the 1970s—where the drive to pursue knowledge could claim additional support from the drive for national security.

The same utilitarian approach drives those who seek to justify harmful experiments on human embryos today. When asked in 1994 whether the National Institutes of Health's [NIH] Human Embryo Research Panel should base its conclusions on the principle that "the end justifies the means," the Panel's chief ethicist quoted the man known as the father of situation ethics, Joseph Fletcher: "If the end doesn't justify the means, what does?" This ethicist later became the chief ethicist for Advanced Cell Technology, the Massachusetts biotechnology company most prominent in the effort to clone human embryos for research purposes. Interestingly, Fletcher himself claimed that the phrase originally came from Nikolai Lenin, who reportedly used it to justify the killing of countless men, women and children in the Russian revolution of 1917.

History provides us with little reason to favor utilitarian thinking about human life—for even judged by its own terms, making moral judgments solely on the basis of consequences has so often had terrible consequences. Because scientists, and the for-profit companies that increasingly support and make use of their research, are always tempted to treat helpless members of the human family as mere means to their ends, the rest of society—including government—*must* supply the urgently needed barrier against unethical exploitation of human beings.

The Moral Status of the Human Embryo

Some will object that one-week-old human embryos, uniquely among all classes of living human organisms, deserve no such protection from destructive experiments. They hold that these embryos, "according to science, bear as much resemblance to a human being as a goldfish."

But this is simply scientific ignorance. Modern embryology textbooks tell us that the initial one-celled zygote is "the beginning of a new human being," and define the "embryo" as "the developing human during its early stages of development."

The continuity of human development from the very beginning, and the reality of the early embryo as a living organism of the human species, has been underscored by recent biological discoveries. Commenting on these new findings, a major science journal concluded that "developmental biologists will no longer dismiss early mammalian embryos as featureless bundles of cells." Political groups may still attempt to do so, of course, but they cannot claim that science is on their side.

While it makes no sense to say that any of us was once a body cell, or a sperm, or an egg, it makes all the sense in the world to say that each of us was once an embryo. For the embryo is the first stage of my life history, the beginning of my continuous development as a human organism. This claim makes the same kind of sense as the claim that I was once a newborn infant, although I do not have any recollection of cognitive or specifically human "experiences" during that stage of life.

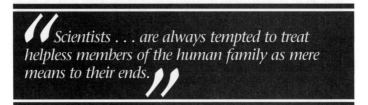

Scientists . . . are always tempted to treat helpless members of the human family as mere means to their ends.

The principle that the embryo deserves recognition and respect as a member of the human family is also already reflected in numerous areas of federal law. At every stage of development, the unborn child in the womb is protected by federal homicide laws as a separate victim when there is a violent attack upon his or her mother. That same child is recognized in federal health regulations as an eligible patient deserving prenatal care. And of course, [since 1996] that same embryo has been protected, in much the same way as other human subjects, from being harmed or killed in federally funded research.

Catholic Moral Teaching

Catholic moral teaching on this issue is very clear. Every human life, from the first moment of existence until natural death, deserves our respect and protection. Human life has *intrinsic* dignity, not only a relative or instrumental value; thus every living member of the human species, including the human embryo, must be treated with the respect due to a human person. We hold further that attempts to make a principled argument as to why embryos need not be respected as persons end up excluding many other members of the human race from this status as well. Any mental or physical ability or characteristic (aside from simple membership in the human race) that one may propose as the deciding factor for "personhood" will be lacking in some people, or held more by some people than by others.

Thus Catholic morality regarding respect for human life, and any secular ethic in agreement with its basic premises, rejects all deliberate involvement with the direct killing of human embryos for research or any other purpose. Such killing is gravely and intrinsically wrong, and no promised beneficial consequences can lessen that wrong. This conviction is also held by many American taxpayers, who should not be forced by government to promote with their tax dollars what they recognize as a direct killing of innocent human persons.

Embryonic Cell Research Destroys Human Life

But even those who do not hold the human embryo to be a full-fledged human person can conclude that embryonic stem cell research is unethical. Many moral wrongs fall short of the full gravity of homicide but are nonetheless seriously wrong. Setting aside "personhood," surely no one prefers funding research that requires destroying human life.

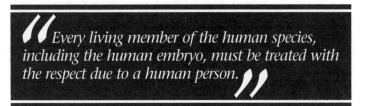

Every living member of the human species, including the human embryo, must be treated with the respect due to a human person.

Four major advisory groups recommending federal policies on human embryo research over the past 23 years have agreed that the destruction of human life is exactly what is at stake in research that involves destroying human embryos. For example, the Ethics Advisory Board to the Department of Health, Education and Welfare concluded in 1979 that the early human embryo deserves "profound respect" as a form of developing human life (though not necessarily "the full legal and moral rights attributed to persons"). The NIH Human Embryo Research Panel agreed in 1994 that "the preimplantation human embryo warrants serious moral consideration as a developing form of human life." In 1999, the National Bioethics Advisory Commission (NBAC) cited broad agreement in our society that "human embryos deserve respect as a form of human life." And in 2002, the National Academy of Sciences acknowledged that "in medical terms," the embryo is a "developing human from fertilization" onwards.

> *Catholic morality . . . rejects all deliberate involvement with the direct killing of human embryos for research or any other purpose.*

What does this respect mean, if it does not mean full and active protection from harm of the kind we extend to human persons? At a minimum, doesn't it mean that we will not use public funds to promote such harm? It is absurd to treat a human life solely as a source of spare parts for other people, and claim that this demonstrates your "respect" for that life. It is equally absurd to fund stem cell research that encourages researchers to destroy human embryos for their cells, and claim that one is not promoting disrespect for the lives of those embryos.

The "Would Have Been Discarded Anyway" Argument

It does not help this argument to claim that the only embryos to be destroyed for research are those who "would have been discarded anyway." The mere fact that some parents discard "excess" embryos creates no argument that the federal government should intervene to assist in their destruction—any more than the fact that many abortions are performed in the U.S. creates an argument that Congress must use its funding power to promote such killing. In fact, Congress has for many years *rejected* arguments that it can fund harmful experiments on unborn children slated for abortion because "they will die soon anyway." The claim that humans who may soon die automatically become fodder for lethal experiments also has ominous implications for condemned prisoners and terminally ill patients. In the final analysis, all of us will die anyway, but that gives no one a right to kill us.

Even on its own amoral terms, that argument also misunderstands the informed consent process for "disposition" of frozen embryos in U.S. fertility clinics. When these clinics produce more embryos in a given cycle than parents need for their immediate reproductive goals, they do indeed freeze the "excess" embryos and ask the parents what should be done with them after a given time. Most clinics offer the options of continuing to preserve the embryos, using them for further reproductive efforts by the couple, donating them to another couple for reproduction, discarding them, or donating them for research. But these are *mutually exclusive options*. For example, it would violate the professional code of the fertility industry to take embryos "to be discarded" and use them for research instead. And among embryos donated for research, no researcher or government official can tell which embryos "would have been discarded" if this option had not been offered.

The Embryonic Human Deserves Respect

The problem with past federal advisory panels is that they have generally failed to give any real content to the notion of "respect" or "serious moral consideration" for the embryonic human. The NIH Human Embryo Research Panel failed miserably in this task. Since the Panel approved a wide array of lethal experiments on human embryos—including some which required specially creating embryos solely to destroy them—even the Panel's own members publicly observed that it had come to use the word "respect" merely as a "slogan" with no moral force.

In the end, the Panel's report was rejected in part by President [Bill] Clinton (who denied funding for experiments involving the creation of embryos for research), and rejected in its entirety by Congress (which enacted the appropriations rider against funding harmful embryo research that remains in law to this day). . . .

Congress should take stock now and realize that the promise of [embryonic stem cell research] is too speculative, and the cost too high. That cost includes the early human lives destroyed now and in the future, the required exploitation of women for their eggs and perhaps for their wombs, and the diversion of finite public resources away from research avenues that offer real reasons for hope for patients with terrible diseases. Let's agree to support avenues to medical progress that we can all live with.

Organizations to Contact

The editors have compiled the following list of organizations concerned with the issues debated in this book. The descriptions are derived from materials provided by the organizations. All have publications or information available for interested readers. The list was compiled on the date of publication of the present volume; the information provided here may change. Be aware that many organizations take several weeks or longer to respond to inquiries, so allow as much time as possible.

ACLU Reproductive Freedom Project
125 Broad St., 18th Fl., New York, NY 10004
(212) 549-2633 • fax: (212) 549-2652
e-mail: RFP@aclu.org • Web site: www.aclu.org/ReproductiveRights

A branch of the American Civil Liberties Union, the project coordinates efforts in litigation, advocacy, and public education to guarantee the constitutional right to reproductive choice. Its mission is to ensure that reproductive decisions will be informed, meaningful, and free of hindrance or coercion from the government. The project disseminates position papers, fact sheets, legislative documents, and publications, including *Abortion Bans: Myths and Facts* and *The ACLU Opposes Federal Restrictions on Mifepristone (RU-486).*

Advocates for Youth
2000 M St. NW, Washington, DC 20036
(202) 419-3420 • fax: (202) 419-1448
e-mail: questions@advocatesforyouth.org
Web site: www.advocatesforyouth.org

Advocates for Youth is dedicated to creating programs and advocating for policies that help young people make informed and responsible decisions about their reproductive and sexual health. It provides information, education, and advocacy to youth-serving agencies and professionals, policy makers, and the media. Among the organization's numerous publications are the fact sheets "Adolescents and Abortion" and "Peer Education: Promoting Healthy Behaviors."

Alan Guttmacher Institute
120 Wall St., 21st Fl., New York, NY 10005
(212) 248-1111 • fax: (212) 248-1951
e-mail: info@guttmacher.org • Web site: www.agi-usa.org

The institute is a reproduction research group that advocates the right to safe and legal abortion. It provides extensive statistical information on abortion and voluntary population control. Its publications include *Perspectives on Sexual and Reproductive Health* and *International Family Planning Perspectives.*

American Life League (ALL)
PO Box 1350, Stafford, VA 22555
(540) 659-4171 • fax: (540) 659-2586
e-mail: office@all.org • Web site: www.all.org

ALL promotes family values and opposes abortion. The organization monitors congressional activities dealing with pro-life issues and provides information on the physical and psychological risks of abortion. It produces educational materials, books, flyers, and programs for pro-family organizations that oppose abortion. The league's publications include the bimonthly magazine *Celebrate Life* and the monthly *Pro-Life Bulletin Board*.

Americans United for Life (AUL)
310 S. Peoria St., Suite 300, Chicago, IL 60607-3534
(312) 492-7234 • fax: (312) 492-7235
e-mail: info@aul.org • Web site: www.unitedforlife.org

AUL promotes legislation to make abortion illegal. The organization operates a library and a legal resource center for such subjects as abortion, infanticide, destructive embryo research, and human cloning. Publications include the articles "Embryo Adoption or Embryo Donation? The Distinction and Its Implications" and "An Authentic Concept of Woman Will Build a Culture of Life."

Catholics for a Free Choice (CFFC)
1436 U St. NW, Suite 301, Washington, DC 20009-3997
(202) 986-6093 • fax: (202) 332-7995
e-mail: cffc@catholicsforchoice.org • Web site: www.cath4choice.org

CFFC supports the right to legal abortion and promotes family planning to reduce the incidence of abortion and to increase women's choice in childbearing and child rearing. It publishes the bimonthly newsletter *Conscience*.

Center for Bio-Ethical Reform (CBR)
PO Box 2339, Santa Fe Springs, CA 90670
(562) 777-9117
e-mail: cbr@cbrinfo.org • Web site: www.cbrinfo.org

CBR opposes legal abortion, focusing its arguments on abortion's moral aspects. Its members frequently address conservative and Christian groups throughout the United States. The center also offers training seminars on fundraising to pro-life volunteers. CBR's audiotapes include "Harder Truth" and "Abortion and the Hereafter." The center's Genocide Awareness Project (GAP) is a traveling photo-mural exhibit that visits university campuses around the country to make students aware of the broader aspects of abortion.

Center for Reproductive Rights
120 Wall St., New York, NY 10005
(917) 637-3600 • fax: (917) 637-3666
e-mail: info@reprorights.org • Web site: www.crlp.org

The center is a nonprofit legal advocacy organization dedicated to promoting and defending women's reproductive rights worldwide. The center advocates for safe and affordable contraception as well as safe and legal abortion for women. Among the center's publications are fact sheets, briefing papers, and articles, including "What If *Roe* Fell?" and "The Women of the World: Laws and Policies Affecting Their Reproductive Lives."

Childbirth by Choice Trust
344 Bloor St. West, Suite 502, Toronto, ON M5S 3A7 Canada
(416) 961-7812 • fax: (416) 961-5771
e-mail: info@cbctrust.com • Web site: www.cbctrust.com

The goal of the Childbirth by Choice Trust is to educate the public about abortion and reproductive choice. It produces educational materials that aim to provide factual, rational, and straightforward information about fertility control issues. The organization's publications include the booklet *Abortion in Law, History, and Religion* and the pamphlets *Unsure About Your Pregnancy? A Guide to Making the Right Decision* and *Information for Teens About Abortion.*

Feminists for Life of America
733 Fifteenth St. NW, Suite 1100, Washington, DC 20005
(202) 737-3352
e-mail: info@feministsforlife.org • Web site: www.feministsforlife.org

This organization is composed of feminists united to secure the right to life, from conception to natural death, for all human beings. It believes that legal abortion exploits women. The group supports a human life amendment that would protect unborn life. It promotes an education campaign titled "Women Deserve Better," which provides women-centered solutions to reduce abortion and protect women's health.

NARAL Pro-Choice America
1156 Fifteenth St. NW, Suite 700, Washington, DC 20005
(202) 973-3000 • fax: (202) 973-3096
e-mail: naral@naral.org • Web site: www.naral.org

NARAL Pro-Choice America works to develop and sustain a pro-choice political constituency in order to maintain the right of all women to legal abortion. The league briefs members of Congress and testifies at hearings on abortion and related issues. Its publications include "Who Decides: A Reproductive Rights Issues Manual" and "Talking About Freedom of Choice."

National Right to Life Committee (NRLC)
512 Tenth St. NW, Washington, DC 20004
(202) 626-8800
e-mail: nrlc@nrlc.org • Web site: www.nrlc.org

NRLC is one of the largest organizations opposing abortion. The committee campaigns against legislation legalizing abortion. It encourages the ratification of a constitutional amendment granting embryos and fetuses the same right to life as living persons, and it advocates alternatives to abortion, such as adoption. NRLC publishes the brochure *When Does Life Begin?* and *Abortion: Some Medical Facts.*

Ontario Consultants on Religious Tolerance (OCRT)
PO Box 128, Watertown, NY 13601-0128
fax: (613) 547-9015
Web site: www.religioustolerance.org

The OCRT is a group that advocates freedom of religion and firmly supports the separation of church and state. Its purpose is to disseminate accurate religious information and expose religious fraud. The group publishes many essays and articles on "hot topics," including "Abortion: All Sides of the Issue" and "The Key Question: When Does Human Personhood Start?"

Planned Parenthood Federation of America (PPFA)
434 W. Thirty-third St., New York, NY 10001
(212) 541-7800 • fax: (212) 245-1845
e-mail: communications@ppfa.org
Web site: www.plannedparenthood.org

PPFA is a national organization that supports people's right to make their own reproductive decisions without governmental interference. It provides contraception, abortion, and family-planning services at clinics located throughout the United States. Among its extensive publications are the fact sheets "Abortion After the First Trimester" and "The Emotional Effects of Induced Abortion."

Religious Coalition for Reproductive Choice (RCRC)
1025 Vermont Ave. NW, Suite 1130, Washington, DC 20005
(202) 628-7700 • fax: (202) 628-7716
e-mail: info@rcrc.org • Web site: www.rcrc.org

RCRC consists of more than thirty Christian, Jewish, and other religious groups committed to helping individuals make decisions concerning abortion in accordance with their consciences. The organization supports abortion rights, opposes antiabortion violence, and educates policy makers and the public about the diversity of religious perspectives on abortion. RCRC publishes booklets, an educational essay series, the quarterly *Faith & Choices* newsletter, and Speak Out series, which includes "Just Say Know!" and "Family Planning: A Moral Good, a Human Right."

United States Conference of Catholic Bishops
3211 Fourth St. NE, Washington, DC 20017-1194
(202) 541-3000 • fax: (202) 541-3054
e-mail: pro-life@usccb.org • Web site: www.nccbuscc.org

The United States Conference of Catholic Bishops, which adheres to the Vatican's opposition to abortion, is the American Roman Catholic bishops' organ for unified action. Through its committee on pro-life activities, it advocates a legislative ban on abortion and promotes state restrictions on abortion, such as parental consent/notification laws and strict licensing laws for abortion clinics. Its pro-life publications include the bulletin "Stem Cell Research and Human Cloning" and the brochure *A People of Life.*

Bibliography

Books

Randy Alcorn — *ProLife Answers to ProChoice Arguments*. Sisters, OR: Multnomah, 2000.

Theresa Burke — *Forbidden Grief: The Unspoken Pain of Abortion*. Springfield, IL: Acorn, 2002.

Guy Condon — *Fatherhood Aborted*. Carol Stream, IL: Tyndale House, 2001.

Gloria Feldt — *Behind Every Choice Is a Story*. Denton: University of North Texas Press, 2004.

N.E.H. Hull and Peter Charles Hoffer — Roe v. Wade: *The Abortion Rights Controversy in American History*. Lawrence: University Press of Kansas, 2001.

Krista Jacob — *Our Choices, Our Lives: Unapologetic Writings on Abortion*. Lincoln, NE: iUniverse, 2004.

Leon R. Kass — *Life, Liberty, and the Defense of Dignity: The Challenge of Bioethics*. San Francisco: Encounter, 2002.

Scott Klusendorf — *Pro-Life 101: A Step-by-Step Guide to Making Your Case Persuasively*. Signal Hill, CA: Stand to Reason, 2002.

Peter Kreeft — *Three Approaches to Abortion: A Thoughtful and Compassionate Guide to Today's Most Controversial Issue*. San Francisco: Ignatius, 2002.

John Charles Kunich — *The Naked Clone: How Cloning Bans Threaten Our Personal Rights*. Westport, CT: Greenwood, 2003.

Jane Maienschein — *Whose View of Life? Embryos, Cloning, and Stem Cells*. Cambridge, MA: Harvard University Press, 2003.

Bill McKibben — *Enough: Staying Human in an Engineered Age*. New York: Henry Holt, 2003.

Erik Patens and Adrienne Asch — *Prenatal Testing and Disability Rights*. Washington, DC: Georgetown University Press, 2000.

James C. Peterson — *Genetic Turning Points*. Grand Rapids, MI: Eerdmans, 2001.

Anna Runkle — *In Good Conscience: A Practical, Emotional, and Spiritual Guide to Deciding Whether to Have an Abortion*. San Francisco: Anna Runkle, 2002.

Alexander Sanger — *Beyond Choice: Reproductive Freedom in the 21st Century*. New York: Public Affairs, 2004.

Gregory Stock — *Redesigning Humans: Our Inevitable Genetic Future*. New York: Houghton Mifflin, 2002.

Periodicals

America — "The Abortion Debate Today," February 16, 2004.

Jennifer Baumgardner — "We're Not Sorry, Charlie," *Nation*, February 2, 2004.

Caitlin Borgmann and Catherine Weiss — "Beyond Apocalypse and Apology: A Moral Defense of Abortion," *Perspectives on Sexual and Reproductive Health*, January/February 2003.

Nell Boyce — "A Law's Fetal Flaw," *U.S. News & World Report*, July 21, 2003.

Monica J. Casper — "Pro-Life Government Decision Is Unfair to American Families," *Seattle Post-Intelligencer*, November 26, 2003.

Eleanor Cooney — "The Way It Was," *Mother Jones*, September/October 2004.

Elden Francis Curtiss — "What Does *Donum Vitae* Teach Pro-Life Americans?" *Celebrate Life*, January/February 2002.

Bryan Dowd and Chris Macosko — "Human Embryo Research: Should We, Just Because We Can?" *St. Paul Pioneer Press*, August 5, 2004.

Jeffrey Drazen — "Inserting Government Between Patient and Physician," *New England Journal of Medicine*, January 8, 2004.

Michael F. Greene and Jeffrey L. Ecker — "Abortion, Health, and the Law," *New England Journal of Medicine*, January 8, 2004.

Stan Guthrie — "Counter Offensive Launched on RU-486," *Christianity Today*, June 11, 2001.

Carolyn A. Johnson — "Life, Death, and Partial-Birth Abortion," *Seattle Post-Intelligencer*, December 5, 2003.

John W. Kennedy — "Complicit Guilt, Explicit Healing: Men Involved in Abortion Are Starting to Find Help," *Christianity Today*, November 2003.

Paul Lauritzen — "Neither Person nor Property: Embryo Research and the Status of the Early Embryo," *America*, March 26, 2001.

Lorraine V. Murray — "The Least of These," *America*, January 22, 2001.

Newsweek — "Cellular Divide," July 9, 2001.

New York Times — "Round One for Women's Health," September 13, 2004.

New York Times	"A Victory for Abortion Rights," June 5, 2004.
Ramesh Ponnuru	"Abortion Now: Thirty Years After *Roe*, a Daunting Landscape," *National Review*, January 27, 2003.
Deborah Rosenberg	"The War over Fetal Rights," *Newsweek*, June 9, 2003.
Rita Rubin	"Early Genetic Testing Allays Fears, Ignites Ethics Debate," *USA Today*, May 26, 2004.
Christine A. Scheller	"A Laughing Child in Exchange for Sin," *Christianity Today*, February 13, 2004.
Lisa Stein	"An Undue Burden," *U.S. News & World Report*, June 14, 2004.
Karyn Strickler	"When Opponents of Legal Abortion Dream . . ." *Off Our Backs*, January/February 2004.
Pamela Pearson Wong	"Abortion's House of Cards," *Family Voice*, January/February 2001.

Internet Sources

| NARAL Pro-Choice America | "The 'Unborn Victims of Violence Act' Is Not the Solution to Domestic Violence," January 1, 2004. www.naral.org. |
| National Right to Life Committee | "Key Facts on the Unborn Victims of Violence Act," April 1, 2004. www.nrlc.org. |

Index